At that time Jefus anfwered, and faid, I giue
thee thākes, o Father, Lord of heauē & earth,
becaufe thou haft hid thefe things from the
wife and men of vnderftanding, and haft opened
them vnto babes.

S. *Matthewe* XI: 25.
(The Geneva Bible, *1560*)

It is therefore the love of liberty that must
free the soul. . . .

Obadiah Holmes, 1675

Baptist Piety

The Last Will & Testimony of Obadiah Holmes

Edited and with Historical Introduction
by

Edwin S. Gaustad

CHRISTIAN
UNIVERSITY
PRESS

A Subsidiary of Christian College Consortium
and Wm. B. Eerdmans Publishing Company
Grand Rapids, Michigan

Copyright © 1978 by Christian College Consortium
11 Dupont Circle, N.W., Washington, D.C. 20036
All rights reserved
Printed in the United States of America

Order from:
Wm. B. Eerdmans Publishing Company
255 Jefferson Ave., S.E., Grand Rapids, Mich. 49503

Library of Congress Cataloging in Publication Data

Holmes, Obadiah, 1606-1682.
    Baptist piety.

    Bibliography: p. 160.
    Includes index.
    1.   Holmes, Obadiah, 1606-1682.   2.   Baptists —
Clergy — Biography.   3.   Clergy — United States — Biography.
I.   Gaustad, Edwin Scott.   II.   Title.
BX6495.H56A33   286'.1'0924 [B]   78-6836
ISBN 0-8028-1747-5

Contents

v

Preface

ONE MAY CONCEDE THAT OBADIAH HOLMES IS NOT A MAJOR figure in American history yet question whether he deserves an obscurity that is almost total. I think that he merits more than that.

The "common" men and women of colonial America are only now coming into their own. Previously, major attention was concentrated on the intellectual and political leaders: the explorers, the warriors, the founders, the statesmen, the Hudsons, Penns, Calverts, Byrds, and Bradfords. Moreover, those who explicitly rejected the established leadership in America — as did Obadiah Holmes — risked not only the pillory and the whip but their place in history as well. Holmes published nothing (though two of his letters were included in another person's publication); he held no political office; he offered no new system of thought; he founded neither a town nor a church; he amassed no great fortune; he acquired no zealous following. He left nothing but a life, and that life has never been told. Holmes has had no biographer, nor did he win so much as a sketch in the *Dictionary of American Biography* or even in the *Annals of the American Pulpit*. He is described in no one's *Graduates of . . .* , for he attended no university.

If he is eclipsed in the broad span of American history, the neglect is hardly corrected in the more narrow scope of religious history. In the general surveys of religion in America, he rates only a line — if that. In his own denomination, the Baptist, he is overshadowed by two better-known, university-educated contemporaries: Roger Williams and

vii

John Clarke. But Williams was a Baptist for only a few months in 1639, and Clarke spent his greatest effort abroad, securing Rhode Island's permanent charter in 1663. Only from Obadiah Holmes, therefore, do we learn in revealing detail about the earliest Baptists in America — their feeling, believing, preaching, quarreling, disciplining, and caring. In Holmes one discovers more about conversion and being born again, more about biblical understanding and evangelical pietism, more about the personal credo and commitment of America's first Baptists than from any other single source. And along the way one comes to know this simple and uneducated man, whose impact nevertheless endures: through his "great posterity" (which includes Abraham Lincoln as well as the notable "Browns of Providence Plantations"); through the continuity of his churchmanship (a thirty-year ministry in Newport); through the example of his suffering (a thirty-stripe flogging in Boston); and through his Testimony, published here for the first time.

Seventeenth-century prose, whether from educated pens or not, is often forbidding and occasionally misleading to a twentieth-century reader. Most of the difficulty is merely mechanical: punctuation, capitalization, spelling, paragraphing, and a marvelously uninhibited use of italics and abbreviations. Spelling (even of proper names) was so casual as to allow for half a dozen variants of a single word in a single work. In Part I, therefore, changes in these "externals" have been made to conform to modern usage. Sometimes the difficulty is verbal: that is, a seventeenth-century word or phrase has a different meaning in the twentieth century or has lost its meaning entirely. In those few instances where it has been necessary to supply other words, these appear within brackets. In Chapters 2 and 3, where some of the primary material has been presented in dialogue form, neither sense nor substance has been altered; a mere shift in tense or personal pronoun is supplied from time to time. Seventeenth-century titles, on the other hand, have been preserved without modification. (With respect to the Testimony itself, see the General Introduction to Part II.)

I always welcome the opportunity to acknowledge the assistance of those who help make scholarship possible and pleasant. Two decades ago I publicly expressed appreciation for a good teacher, Edmund S. Morgan. The intervening years have diminished neither my debt nor my gratitude; he remains a good teacher who demands even more of himself than of others. And to another good teacher, Sidney E. Mead, I owe much. While I was never "his" student in any formal sense, I have gained more from chance encounters, hallway conversations, and helpful letters than one has any right to expect. I must also express the deepest appreciation to the Newport Historical Society, and especially to Mrs. Gladys Bolhouse. Not only were the Society's unique materials made available to me for research, but the Society generously gave permission for the publication here of the Testimony, the will, and the inventory. I have also been aided by the staffs of the Massachusetts Historical Society, the Rhode Island Historical Society, the Seventh Day Baptist Historical Society, the Chetham's Library in Manchester, and Regents Park College in Oxford.

Finally, I am grateful to the University of California, Riverside for a term of sabbatical leave, as well as for constant and uncomplaining assistance from an excellent library staff.

E. S. G.

Chronology
Obadiah Holmes

July; arrested, tried, and imprisoned; publicly whipped in early September

1652   letters published in Clarke's *Ill Newes*; assumed leadership of Newport church in Clarke's absence

1655   enrolled as freeman; served on grand jury

1656   served as commissioner for the town; Six Principle Baptists withdraw from the Newport church

1657   divided his own land from farm owned jointly with Smith, Devel, and Mann; joined with Samuel Hubbard in a mission to the Dutch on Long Island

1658   continued to serve on several juries

1662   witnessed land sale by Indian chief to Roger Williams and others

1667-71 period of disaffection from the Newport church

1668   detained by Charlestown constables in the home of Thomas Goold

1671   played a major role in the Seventh-Day Baptist schism

1672   probably attended Roger Williams' public dispute with the Quakers in Newport in August

1675   wrote the Testimony

1676   became sole spokesman for the Newport church following the deaths of Torrey, Clarke, and Lucar; appointed to advise Rhode Island General Assembly

1681   deeded the farm to his son Jonathan and drew up last will

1682   died, October 15

PART I
Historical Introduction

CHAPTER I

"Like a Wave Tossed Up and Down" (1607-1650)

OBADIAH HOLMES WAS BORN IN NORTHERN ENGLAND, NEAR Manchester, around the year 1607 — some four years before the King James Version of the Bible was published or the first permanent Baptist congregation was planted on English soil. At the time of his birth, the Protestant Reformation was still less than a century old and England's separation from Rome little more than half of that. Following the death of Henry VIII in 1547, England experienced extreme religious turbulence in the brief but bloody reigns of Edward VI and Mary I. During the long reign of Elizabeth I (1558-1603) the Church of England struggled to define its own identity and determine its specific course. With the accession of James I in 1603, Puritans within that national church harbored high hopes for a more thorough-going reform of England's established religion: that is, they hoped that the continental Reformation — especially in its Calvinist manifestation — would more powerfully pervade and shape the Church of England.

These hopes were quickly dashed by a Stuart king who saw the unity and tranquility of the national church as essential to the unity and security of his kingdom. Nor did James show any sympathy toward those Puritans who in 1605 petitioned him for the right "to assemble together somewhere publicly to the service and worship of God, to use and enjoy peaceably among ourselves alone the whole exercise of God's worship and of church government . . . without any tradition of men whatsoever, according only to the specification of God's written word and no otherwise. . . ." The humble petitioners likewise noted, in words that summarized neatly much of England's prior religious history, "that we your Majesty's sworn loyal subjects . . . have been now a great many years grievously afflicted and molested, defamed, impoverished, yea and otherwise extraordinarily punished, for no other cause in the world, but only for our conscience. . . ."[1]

This was the England into which Obadiah Holmes was born, an England that would continue to be torn by religious persecutions and harassments, by "popish plots" on the one hand and "seditious separatism" on the other, a nation of regicide and revolution, of banishment and exile. During this turbulent post-Reformation period England changed its religion like some men change their clothes, said Roger Williams, and that he considered its "sinful shame."[2] Between the first Act of Uniformity (passed in 1549) and the Act of Toleration (adopted in 1689), England drew blood and breath from thousands of Catholics or Protestants or heretics or dawdlers who simply neglected to change their religious garments in time.

Holmes' birthplace lay in the rural area of Reddish, five miles southeast of the center of Manchester. The closest village, Stockport, consisted of only a few hundred souls, and Manchester itself, long before the giantism imposed by the Industrial Revolution, had a mere two thousand.[3] The Reddish farmland straddled the boundary between Cheshire and Lancashire, those ancient "palatine counties" occupied by the Roman armies sixteen centuries earlier and the stage for much subsequent British history, both secular and sacred. During the Middle Ages and especially after the Norman conquest, these northwestern counties saw great churches and religious houses rise in their midst: the abbey of Furness (1127), the Saxon abbey of St. Werburg in Chester (later becoming that city's cathedral in 1541), the Collegiate Church of Manchester itself, founded in 1422 and established as the Manchester Cathedral in 1847. These and many other abbeys, priories, chantries, and religious hospitals were dissolved by Henry VIII in 1536 and 1539, actions that sent waves of shock throughout England but especially in Lancashire and Cheshire, where Roman Catholicism was quite strong. Even after Henry, these two counties remained as centers of Catholic resistance to acts of national religious conformity. Lancashire was described in 1574 as "the very sink of Popery where more unlawful acts have been committed and more unlawful persons held secret than in any other part of the realm."[4]

But, remarkably enough, these two counties also seethed with Puritan preaching and agitation, especially in and around Manchester, and especially in the generation immediately preceding and immediately following the birth of Obadiah Holmes. In the huge diocese of Chester, Manchester was the major Puritan center. Puritan clergy dominated many of the leading parish churches, while the Puritan laity exercised an even more determinative influence in the numerous small and newly created chapels. As an economic and trading center, Manchester radiated its influence — commercial and religious — throughout all of the surrounding area. "Manchester was clearly the largest, most prosperous, most economically developed and most puritan town" of the region.[5]

In the reign of Mary (1553-1558), two of Protestantism's most powerfully symbolic martyrs claimed this part of England as home. The lives and deaths of George Marsh and John Bradford, both natives of Lancashire, filled dozens of pages in John Foxe's much celebrated and much read *Book of Martyrs*. That book, published in 1563, and the Bishop's Bible, authorized in 1568, were both read publicly in church to Elizabethan Englishmen. Obadiah Holmes, like other natives of the Manchester region, would have been especially moved by the spiritual heroics of his land's very own severely persecuted, bravely dying martyrs. George Marsh, arrested and endlessly examined concerning his views of the sacrament of communion, wrote to his fellow Puritans in Manchester on August 30, 1554:

> Consider also the wicked of this world [who] . . . will fight with sword and weapons, and put themselves in danger of imprison-

ment and hanging. So much as virtue is better than vice, and God mightier than the devil, so much ought we to excel them in this our spiritual battle.

And seeing, brethren, it hath pleased God to set me and that most worthy minister of Christ, John Bradford, your country-man, in the forefront of this battle where, for the time, is most danger, I beseech you all, in the bowels of Christ, to help us and all other of our fellow-soldiers standing in like perilous place, with your prayers to God for us, that we may quit ourselves like men in the Lord, and give some example of boldness and con-stancy mingled with patience in the fear of God. . . .

Eight months later George Marsh was led from prison "with a lock upon his feet" to the place of execution just outside the Roman walls surrounding the city of Chester. There, as John Foxe related in a passage many Protestants knew virtually by heart,

he was chained to the post, having a number of faggots under him, and a thing made like a firkin with pitch and tar in the same over his head; and by reason the fire was unskillfully made, and that the wind did drive the same to and fro, he suffered great extremity in his death, which notwithstanding he abode very patiently.[6]

Three months later, in July 1555, John Bradford suffered a like fate. But before the torch was set, he too wrote to his sympathizers in Manchester, with even a special greeting to those in the tiny village of Stockport (February 11, 1555):

Therefore, my dear hearts in the Lord, turn you, turn you to the Lord your Father, to the Lord your Saviour, to the Lord your Comforter. Oh! why do you stop your ears, and harden your hearts today, when you hear His voice by me your poorest brother? Oh! forget not how the Lord hath showed himself true, and me his true preacher, by bringing to pass these plagues which at my mouth you oft heard me preach of before they came: specially when I treated of Noah's flood and when I preached of the 23rd chapter of St. Matthew's Gospel on St. Stephen's day, the last time that I was with you . . . you have been warned, and warned again, by me in preaching, by me in burning.

In the town of Smithfield, near the Scottish border, Bradford was tied to the post as bundles of dry twigs were stacked around him. "Earnestly exhorting the people to repent and return to Christ, and sweetly comforting the godly young springal [lad, John Leaf] of nineteen or twenty years old [who] was burned with him," Bradford cheerfully "ended his painful life, to live with Christ."[7]

Into this milieu, one in which it was hardly necessary to argue that religion was a matter of life and death, Obadiah Holmes was born as the second son of Robert Holmes and Catherine Johnson Holmes (the family name was at the time more commonly spelled Hulmes or Hullme). Baptized in Didsbury Chapel (one of those chapels with Puritan tendencies) on March 18, 1610,[8] Obadiah grew up in a farm family of eight or nine children. Although Robert Holmes was a farmer of modest means, he managed to send three of his sons to Oxford; but Obadiah was not among them.[9] Since Obadiah Holmes later became a glassmaker and a weaver, it may well be that "bookish" interest was minimal in his early years. According to his own later account (see below, Part II, Section A), serious interests of almost any kind were minimal in his youthful days. He was, he noted in his Testimony, "the most rebellious child" of all, who hearkened neither "to counsel nor any instruction, for from a child I minded nothing but folly and vanity. . . ." Though such superlatives of sinfulness were part of the accepted form of conversion narratives of the time, they do suggest at the least that Obadiah did not consider himself a model child and therefore, perhaps, not a suitable subject for an expensive college education. Instead, Obadiah was probably apprenticed to glass workers in Stockport.[10]

When this second Holmes son was still quite young, James I issued his Declaration of Sports in 1617. Aimed explicitly at Lancashire, through which the king had journeyed on his return from Scotland, James personally rebuked "some Puritans and precise people" for their narrow and restrictive attitude toward Sunday. For the Puritans, Sunday was a day of worship and rest, not of amusement and recreation. For the king, Sunday — at least that portion of it "after the ending of all divine service" — was a time for "all lawful recreation and exercise." Dancing, leaping, vaulting,

"Maypoles" and "Whitsun ales" — all were wholly appropriate. James offered two quite logical reasons for their appropriateness: (1) people would then see that "honest mirth" was perfectly consistent with true religion; and (2) exercise and recreation would make bodies "more able for war."[11] The declaration was, of course, far more than a casual comment on the virtues of physical education or on the merits of making a joyful noise unto the Lord; it was the royal pleasure. And in this instance what pleased the king did, in the minds of the Puritans, very much displease the Lord. In this as in other royal decrees, James made the alternatives simple and clear: conform or depart. How Obadiah responded to all of this we do not know, but if his acknowledged "folly and vanity" was more than a literary artifice, then he, like his king, probably preferred the Whitsun ales to the Puritan scowls.[12]

James was succeeded in 1625 by Charles I, who maintained his father's policy and reissued the declaration "concerning lawful sports" on October 18, 1633.[13] But by that time actions even more disturbing to the Puritan party had been taken. Charles appointed the strongly anti-Puritan William Laud as Bishop of London in 1628 and, then, as Archbishop of Canterbury in 1633. Under Laud's heavy hand, Puritan unrest increased sharply as James' hard alternatives — "conform or depart" — became harder still. If conscience could not be free in England, what in the world could one do, where in the world should one go?

During much of this period, Obadiah Holmes underwent a prolonged spiritual crisis (see below, Part II, Section A). "My spirit was like a wave tossed up and down," he later wrote, as he tried moral reformation, sought spiritual counsel, questioned his own sincerity, read the Bible without finding comfort, prayed with fervor and frequency, and denounced conformity in religion as "only superstition and a name." "Yet for all that I had no rest in my soul. . . ." Like other twice-born men, Holmes found the long dark night of the soul to be of such duration and agony that it was almost beyond enduring. The more he listened to the preaching of the Word, the more that Word seemed aimed against him: "The wicked shall be turned to hell." The more he confessed his sins and promised publicly to forsake them, the more he "judged it was all done in hypocrisy." He wrote: "Then Satan let fly at me and told me it was too late for return, for there was no hope for me." The spiritual struggle even began to have its physiological effect as Holmes grew weak and despondent; "yet for ease and comfort I turned over every stone. . . ."

Some four or five years before his mother's death in 1630, Obadiah Holmes had revelled in his waywardness and skepticism, thinking "it best when I could do the most wickedness." But then he "began to bethink what counsel my dear parents had given me, many a call, many a time with tears and prayers; my rebellion to my honored parents then looked me in the open face." His mother's illness and death proved a turning point: "It struck me that my disobedient acts caused her death, which forced me to confess the same to her — my evil ways." Still, the struggles went on, as that peace which passes all understanding seemed to come near and then teasingly elude him once more.

Two months after his mother's death, Obadiah Holmes took Catherine Hyde as his wife. They were married in Manchester's Collegiate Church on November 20, 1630.[14] An infant son, born in June 1633, died soon after and was buried in the village cemetery in Stockport.

Meanwhile, Laud's public campaign against Puritanism intensified, notably so in northern England. Puritan preachers were silenced, conformity was demanded, bishops and archbishops were alerted to root out heresy and punish schism. When Archbishop Neile of York visited the sprawling diocese of Chester in 1633, he bristled at what he found:

> . . . the Book of Common Prayer is so neglected and abused in most places by chopping, changing, altering, omitting and adding at the ministers' own pleasure, as if they are not bound to the form prescribed. In sundry places the Book of Common Prayer was so unregarded that many knew not how to read the service according to the Book.[15]

In Manchester itself, the leading Puritan bookseller, Thomas Smith, was arrested in 1638 and charged with selling "divers

Scottish and other schismatical books, containing in them divers bitter invectives and railings against the government and discipline of the Church of England."[16] Holmes' own spiritual travail was but a reflection of the uncertainty and suffering of a whole generation of English pilgrims. The decade of the 1630s so disheartened England's Puritans that they left their homeland in shipload after shipload to create a newer and purer England far away from Laud and his minions. These were the years of the Great Migration, as later historians would call it; and these were the years when Obadiah Holmes also "adventured the danger of the seas to come to New England."

Holmes and his wife probably sailed from Preston (just north of Liverpool), down the River Ribble, across the Irish Sea, and into the open Atlantic.[17] They arrived in Boston harbor most likely in the summer or early fall of 1638, when some twenty ships, all loaded with immigrants, yielded up their human cargo: "at least three thousand persons," John Winthrop noted in his Journal, so many at one time that "they were forced to look out new plantations."[18] In three years, however, the population boom was over and momentous changes were occurring in England. Parliament began, wrote Winthrop, "setting upon a general reformation both of church and state . . . [which] caused all men to stay in England in expectation of a new world. . . ." But for Obadiah and Catherine Holmes, as they stepped off their tiny ship the new world lay before them.

By January of 1639 these two new pilgrims were in Salem; on the twenty-first of that month Holmes received one acre of land for a house and a promise of ten more acres "to be laid out by the town." Other smaller grants of land were made to the couple during the next three years,[19] as the young Salem settlement (about a thousand inhabitants at this time) sought to encourage Holmes and his co-workers in the development of what may have been the first glass factory in North America.[20] Glass-making continued in Salem for three or four decades, though capital there as elsewhere in colonial America was too scarce to permit any impressive development. In addition to his labors as a glassman, Holmes performed other duties befitting the good citizen and neighbor: he surveyed and set boundaries for the land of another citizen in February 1643; he accepted appointment by the town in September 1644 to cut and gather firewood for the church elders; in January 1645 he witnessed the will and appraised the estate of the "widow Margaret Pease"; and he often served on juries during his years of residence in Salem.[21]

In March of 1640, Obadiah and Catherine Holmes became members of the Salem church whose pastor, the remarkable Hugh Peter, was to be executed in England in 1660 for treason. Before Peter's stay in Salem, the church had been subjected to the stormy leadership of Roger Williams, both in 1631 and again between 1633 and 1635. Williams had offended not only Salem but all of Massachusetts Bay by asserting repeatedly that the Congregational churches of New England must separate themselves completely from the impure, bishop-ridden Church of England; that the civil magistrates had no authority over purely religious activity (the "first table" of the ten commandments); and that the Massachusetts charter was null and void because no one had bothered to purchase the land from the Indians. Their patience exhausted, the Bay authorities banished Roger Williams in October 1635, but promised to allow him to remain in the colony until spring — since winter was at hand and his wife was pregnant. He could stay, however, only if he kept silent and did not draw others to his radical and thoroughly unnerving opinions. But silence never came easy to Roger Williams. Therefore, by January of 1636 he found it necessary to flee Salem, making his way on foot to the headwaters of Narragansett Bay, where he negotiated with the Indians for some land and founded the town of Providence, in a "sense of God's merciful Providence to me in my distress." The destinies of Roger Williams and Obadiah Holmes were to cross later in Rhode Island; but even in Salem the church covenant that Holmes signed had been expanded in an effort to ward off the evils that might be inflicted by future troublemakers and schismatics.[22]

Salem's original church covenant, adopted in 1629, had a classic simplicity: "We covenant with the Lord and one with another; and do bind ourselves in the presence of God to walk together in all His ways, according as He is pleased to reveal Himself unto us in His blessed word of truth." By 1636, however, the church was obliged to enlarge on a few points. The members now pledged themselves to avoid "all jealousies, suspicions, backbitings, censurings, provokings, secret risings of spirit" against fellow church members, promising rather "to bear and forbear, give and forgive" as Christ had taught. The congregation also agreed to avoid "distempers and weaknesses in public," covenanting "to carry ourselves in all lawful obedience to those that are over us in Church or Commonweal. . . ."[23] Salem, which had earlier shown some disturbing tendencies toward an independent spirit, now placed itself in or under stronger hands in Boston. After those difficult days with Roger Williams, the church wanted only to be a part of the colony's Puritan and Congregational establishment. And after the difficult days in England, Obadiah Holmes also appeared ready to accept a new conformity in his new world.

For example, he dutifully brought to church for baptism the children born to him and Catherine while in Salem: Martha on May 3, 1640; Samuel on March 20, 1642; and Obadiah, Jr., on June 9, 1644.[24] Moreover, in the year that he himself joined the Salem church, Holmes took one Richard Fowler to court "for reproachful speeches against the ordinance of God"; on March 30, 1641, Fowler was fined forty shillings for his untoward behavior.[25] Nonetheless, however dutiful and conformist Holmes' behavior appeared in Salem, as early as 1643 he was looking around for some other land and perhaps for some other ecclesiastical order as well.

Before October of 1643, Obadiah Holmes had taken an option on land in the newly created community of Rehoboth (or Seekonk), forty miles south of Boston and only ten miles east of Providence. Rehoboth lay within the patent of Plymouth Colony, outside the direct jurisdiction of the Massachusetts Bay authorities. By January 1645, Rehoboth's first settlers declared Holmes' new land — and that of seventeen other persons — to be forfeited for "not fencing or not removing their families" to the new town as they had been instructed to do fifteen months before.[26] Holmes, who perhaps did have difficulty selling his property in Salem or proving his clear title thereto,[27] managed to sell his holdings in Salem by 1645, removing himself and his family to Rehoboth the same year — apparently in time to recover the forfeited land.[28]

In Rehoboth, Obadiah Holmes was elevated to the status of freeman in 1648: that is, as a propertied citizen in good standing he held the right to vote and accepted the obligation to serve, when called upon, in a variety of civic duties.[29] One of those duties, that of surveying, fell again to Holmes in 1647, when Governor Thomas Dudley (of Massachusetts Bay) appointed him, along with Zachary Rhoades and William Carpenter, to survey the extent of the damage to the Indians' crops "done by the English now living at Shawomet" in Rhode Island. The thankless task proved abortive, however, for those colonists allegedly responsible for trampling through the natives' corn refused to recognize Dudley's appointees. Furthermore, these colonists argued, if damages were to be assessed, someone should begin to put a price on all the damage and hardship they had suffered at the hands of the Indians. This minor episode, one among many, hinted at deep and smoldering resentments that would explode a generation later in costly, bloody conflict.[30]

Settled originally by fifty-eight planters in 1643, Rehoboth had grown only slightly by the time Holmes and his family arrived.[31] The village of about three hundred inhabitants had a single church, presided over by Samuel Newman, an English Puritan who had come to Massachusetts the same year Holmes did. Both Obadiah and Catherine participated in this church's public worship. Newman, very early on the scene, had given the town its name (meaning "broad places" or "room"): "For now the Lord has made room for us, and we shall be fruitful in the land" (Gen. 26:22).[32]

But though the land was wide and barely settled, New-

13

man and Holmes found themselves in sharp contention. In October 1649, Holmes took Newman to court, suing him for £100 for slander because the latter had said that Holmes had taken a false oath in court. Obadiah Holmes won the case; but he indicated that he would be satisfied if Newman publicly admitted that the charge was false and paid both the court costs (£1 and 6 pence) and the witness fee (12 shillings to William Carpenter).[33] Newman acknowledged that he had spoken on hearsay only, paid the costs, and the brief squall was calmed.

In a contest more severe and more controverted, Holmes complained against Newman for acting arbitrarily if not autocratically in the church's own internal affairs. In a membership of twenty-three, a vote of admonition against one of the brothers was passed with only seven members voting. This action struck Holmes as both inappropriate and unacceptable.

> . . . when I heard of it, I went to Mr. Newman and told him of the evil which he and the other six had done. He told me they were the Church Representatives, and if four of them had done it, it [would still have] been a Church Act. When this came to the congregation with much ado, he got five more to himself; and then they were twelve, and we eleven. Then, they owned themselves to be the Church, and so began to deal with me for saying they had abused the Church and had took from them their power. Whereupon I told them that I should renounce them and not have any more fellowship with them till either they saw their sin, or I further light. . . .[34]

Thomas Cobbet, a pastor in Lynn, Massachusetts, provided further detail concerning this incident — as well as a sharply opposing point of view. The object of all this controversy, Cobbet wrote, was "a certain brother, J. D. [John Daggett?]," who was charged "for offensive carriage" and "voted a delinquent by the Church, of which Obadiah was one." Now, this matter brewed and bubbled for "many days and times" until one Sunday evening after services Samuel Newman "consented to stay about the business." Obadiah Holmes and five others were present in that meeting at the beginning but left before the admonition was voted. They left

14

without asking permission to leave, Cobbet pointed out, and without indicating any disapproval of the matter at hand. Actually, Cobbet reported, fifteen of the twenty-three members were present from the start, including "J. D." himself. Concerning those that were absent, "four of the brethren kept cattle," a fifth was ill, a sixth was employed thirty miles away, and a seventh was in England. How ridiculous, under those circumstances, to charge irregularity or tyranny, or to declare — as Holmes did publicly the following Sunday in church — that if seven members can so act, "then four, three, two and then a Bishop, a Pope." These expressions, Cobbet added, "were very offensive for matter and manner, both to the Town as well as to the Church." Besides, Cobbet ingenuously asked, what difference do numbers make? "Is not the promise of Christ with those few, though but a few (Matthew 18) even with two or three met together in His name about His work?"[35]

Writing two or three years after the event, Holmes on the one hand and Cobbet on the other offered recollections and detail that simply will not mesh. And while Holmes may have been self-serving in his account, Cobbet was clearly on the attack in his. Holmes pretends to an innocence which he in fact does not possess, Cobbet observed, especially when, like Job, he inquires, "Who ever reproved me of evil?"[36] A lot of people, that's who, said Cobbet, including your own wife. Holmes "was often reproved publicly for divers scandals," for such matters as offensive speeches "respecting a Sister" and "uncircumspect drinking of wine." Once, Holmes was even described before many witnesses as the "arrantest rogue and rascal in a country." There was reproof aplenty, as well as much private counsel, but nothing brought reform in Holmes' misguided and obstinate behavior. Despite the good efforts of good people, concluded Cobbet, Holmes continued to be proud and peremptory, to talk back both to elder and teacher, to disrupt the peace and love of the church, and finally to absent himself from the ordinances of the Rehoboth church.[37]

So, what was the truth concerning this unhappy discord? The truth is that far more lay below the surface than a mere argument about democratic procedures in the church or virtuous behavior in its members. A greater horror lurked like a giant iceberg, waiting to sink any vessel that incautiously came too near. That horror was Anabaptism. During the four years that Obadiah Holmes lived in Rehoboth, anxieties related to the growth of Baptist sentiments multiplied throughout Massachusetts. In 1644, Winthrop noted in his Journal that "Anabaptistry increased and spread in the country, which occasioned the magistrates at the last court to draw an order for banishing such as continued obstinate after due conviction."[38] The law for the obstinate, as finally formulated and published in 1645, read as follows:

> Forasmuch as experience has plentifully & often proved that since the first arising of the Anabaptists, about a hundred years since, they have been the incendiaries of commonwealths & the infectors of persons in main matters of religion, and the troublers of churches in all places where they have been, and that they who have held the baptizing of infants unlawful have usually held other errors or heresies together therewith . . . & whereas divers of this kind have, since our coming into New England, appeared among ourselves, some whereof have (as others before them) denied the ordinance of magistracy & the lawfulness of making war, & others the lawfulness of magistrates & their inspection into any breach of the first table — which opinions, if they should be connived at by us, are like to be increased among us, & so must necessarily bring guilt upon us, infection & trouble to the churches & hazard to the whole commonwealth;
>
> It is ordered & agreed, that if any person or persons within this jurisdiction shall either openly condemn or oppose the baptizing of infants, or go about secretly to seduce others from the approbation or use thereof, or shall purposely depart the congregation at the administration of the ordinance, or shall deny the ordinance of magistracy, or their lawful right or authority to make war, or to punish the outward breaches of the first table, & shall appear to the Court willfully & obstinately to continue therein after due time & means of conviction, every such person or persons shall be sentenced to banishment.[39]

Thus the Bay Colony revealed its horror no less than its contempt of those who would reject either infant baptism or civil power in religious affairs. This law set the stage for Obadiah Holmes' real and lasting difficulties in Rehoboth; at the same time, it shaped his destiny — and that of much of New England besides.

The increase of "Anabaptistry" was no figment of Winthrop's imagination or of the court's. Since Roger Williams had carved out a refuge around Providence in 1636 and John Clarke a similar sanctuary in Newport in 1639, Baptists and other dissenters had found a free and fertile soil in which to grow and — unless something were swiftly done — propagate. By the middle of the 1640s, Baptists had reached into the soft underbelly of Massachusetts, especially into the territory controlled by the more tolerant (or less vigilant) Plymouth Colony. In 1649, Roger Williams observed in a letter to John Winthrop, Jr.:

> At Seekonk [Rehoboth] a great many have lately concurred with Mr. John Clarke and our Providence men about the point of a new Baptism and the manner by dipping; and Mr. John Clarke has been there lately (and Mr. [Mark] Lucar) and has dipped them.[40]

Baptist zeal in Rhode Island was immeasurably heightened by a direct infusion of English Baptists from abroad. Mark Lucar had been a member of John Spilsbury's Baptist church in England, the first Calvinist or Particular Baptist church to be formed there (1633). Arrested and imprisoned a while in London for his nonconformity, Lucar along with others became convinced in about 1641 that immersion or "dipping" was the only proper form of baptism. (Prior to this time, English Baptists had concerned themselves more with the *subject* of baptism — i.e., that it should be an adult or believer rather than a mere passive infant — than with its *mode* — i.e., sprinkling or pouring or dipping.) Lucar arrived in Newport around 1648 and probably introduced "dipping" to the church there almost immediately, and to the disaffected group in Rehoboth shortly thereafter.[41] This was the "new baptism" of which Williams spoke, an innovation that brought conflict and irritation to the Puritans but brought peace and serenity, at last, to Obadiah Holmes.

17

The travail of rebirth could be more prolonged and painful than even that first breaking forth from the mother's womb; and during those last turbulent months in Rehoboth, Holmes was born anew. "It pleased the Father of Light," Holmes wrote two years later, "after a long continuance of mine in death and darkness to cause life and immortality to be brought to light in my soul." One facet of that light permitted him to perceive, through the eyes of faith, that those who believed in a Christ who died that men might live "should yield up themselves to hold forth a lively consimilitude or likeness unto his death, burial and resurrection by that ordinance of baptism."[42] But even brighter facets of light shone upon him. After so many years of so much struggle, Holmes finally saw the absurd futility of his own constant striving, the utter inadequacy of his own merit or worthiness; he saw the simple but saving truth "that there is no preparative necessary to obtain Christ. . . ." Nothing can be done by man; there is nothing that he can do to bring down salvation from heaven to earth. For what has to be done has already been done — and done by God, not by man. At last Holmes saw, or better, "God at last brought me to consider," that there is only one ground, one hope, one promise for salvation: "His own love to poor lost man." There it was, so obvious yet so furtive, so winsome yet so repeatedly rejected. The time had now come to let "free grace . . . have its free course," to be removed "from the covenant of works to the covenant of grace," to be no more "like a wave tossed up and down." Now he could speak of "that ever-rested one, my own heart. . . ."[43] Baptized with the "new baptism" along with eight others, Obadiah Holmes took the irrevocable step toward separation or schism from New England's official way.[44] The spiritual trials were over, the civil struggles would now begin.

For in colonial Massachusetts the affairs of church were inevitably also the affairs of state. In June 1650, a four-barreled petition leveled against Obadiah Holmes and others came before Plymouth's General Court. One section of the petition bore the signature of thirty-five citizens of Rehoboth, another included the names of all Plymouth ministers except

18

two, a third came from a neighboring church, and the fourth emanated from Boston's own interested court. "The Adversary," said Holmes, "cast a flood against us." The "adversary," moreover, was prompted. Boston, long restless and concerned about Plymouth's more relaxed attitude toward novelty and dissent, had written a letter to Plymouth's General Court the previous October, urging the latter to take more vigorous action than they had been noted for in the past. We had counted on you, said the Boston Court, to stamp out Anabaptists the moment you spotted them, to lead the "erring men into the right way."

> But now, to our great grief, we are credibly informed that your patient bearing with such men has produced another effect: namely, the multiplying and increasing of the same errors, and we fear maybe of other errors also, if timely care be not taken to suppress the same. Particularly we understand that within these few weeks there have been at Seekonk [Rehoboth] thirteen or fourteen persons rebaptized (a swift progress in one town!). Yet we hear not of any effectual restriction intended thereabouts . . . we earnestly intreat you to take care as well of the suppressing of errors as of the maintenance of truth, God equally requiring the performance of both at the hands of Christian magistrates. . . . Consider our interest. . . . The infection of such diseases, being so near us, are likely to spread into our jurisdiction. . . .[45]

Under such prodding, the Plymouth Court gathered its evidence and heard the charges. The burden of the petition was that the dissident group (Holmes and eight others) had set up a separate and irregular church meeting in opposition to the orderly, approved, and established congregation led by the Reverend Mr. Samuel Newman. All such schismatical activity, the petitioners urged, should cease forthwith. The court responded, mildly enough, by ordering the group (in Holmes' words) "to desist, and neither to ordain officers, nor to baptize, nor to break bread together, nor yet to meet upon the first day of the week. . . ."[46] Three of the men who had earlier been "bound one for another in the sum of ten pounds apiece"— Holmes, Joseph Torrey, and William Carpenter — now heard the sentence of the court. Holmes and Torrey stood fast, vowing to continue to meet, break bread, and baptize,

but the faith of William Carpenter rested on a "sandy foundation," which collapsed before the wind, rain, and flood of
men's opposition.[47]

On October 2, 1650, Holmes, Torrey, and eight others
were ordered back into the Plymouth Court "for the continuing of a meeting upon the Lord's day from house to house,
contrary to the order of this Court enacted June 12, 1650."[48]
In addition to the two named above, the rebellious group
included Edward Smith, William Devel, James Mann (and
each man's wife), the wife of Joseph Torrey, and John Hazel.
No sandy foundations were uncovered here, for the entire
group, with the exception of John Hazel, maintained contact
and communion in Rhode Island for many years after. (Hazel,
an older man, crossed the path of Obadiah Holmes again only
briefly, but that most poignantly.[49]) The court's verdict from
this October 2 confrontation has not survived. But whatever
the decision of the moment, the long-term verdict was clear:
Holmes and his followers would find peace neither in
Plymouth Colony nor in Massachusetts Bay. Where now did
God lead, where now could they go?

The "new baptism" had come from Newport, from the
island of Aquidneck, where not only was land to be found but
also liberty of conscience. From the point of view of Obadiah
Holmes, it made sense once more to sell house and lands and
to move family and possessions to a colony where courts did
not trespass over that boundary that marked a man's private
faith. It also made perfect sense to Cotton Mather that such
an Anabaptist sect would sink itself into that cesspool called
Rhode Island. He noted in his *Ecclesiastical History of New
England:*

> If I should now launch forth into a narrative of the marvelous
> lewd things which have been done and said by the giddy sec-
> taries of this island, I confess the matter would be agreeable
> enough to the nature and the design of a church history, and for a
> warning unto all to take heed how they forsake the word of God
> and His ordinances . . . but the merriment arising from the
> ridiculous and extravagant occurrences therein would not be
> agreeable to the gravity of such a history.

20

So Cotton Mather contented himself with the scandalized observation that "there never was held such a variety of religions together on so small a spot of ground" as in Rhode Island: "Antinomians, Familists, Anabaptists, Anti-sabbatarians, Arminians, Socinians, Quakers, Ranters — everything in the world but Roman Catholics and real Christians. . . ."[50]

When Obadiah Holmes left Rehoboth, he probably thought that he had left behind for good the Cotton Mathers, the meddling civil magistrates, the condescending clergy, the intrusive and insolent laws. Newport seemed far away from all this — but it was not far enough.

CHAPTER 2

"Baptized in Afflictions by your Hands" (1651-1652)

OBADIAH HOLMES TOOK ONE TENTATIVE STEP ONTO HISTORY'S wider stage in 1651. In that year the structures of the New England way clashed directly with the turbulence of a Rhode Island way, with results that reverberated all the way to London and back. The contrary forces were neither immovable nor irresistible; each had its limits, and each its measure of victory and of defeat. "The event" of 1651 surely had its own inherent drama, but how that event was interpreted is the stuff — and the power — of history.

On July 16, 1651, John Clarke, John Crandall, and Obadiah Holmes journeyed from Newport into Massachusetts, coming to the town of Lynn on the nineteenth of that month. Clarke, one of the founders of Newport (1639) and of the dissenting "church of Christ" there, had embraced Baptist views by at least 1644.[1] John Crandall, whose son had married a daughter of the notorious Samuel Gorton,[2] likewise proclaimed "believer's baptism" to be the gospel-ordered way for sinners to enter into Christ's visible church; Crandall later became a Seventh Day Baptist.[3] And Holmes, as we have seen, had become a Baptist only two years before this trek to Lynn. So all three men were evangelists in a new cause, with the vigor and zeal of recent converts; such zeal might well provoke a counterthrust of equal force designed to eradicate, if possible, this virulent and suddenly expanding sectarian madness.

The purpose of the visit, narrowly conceived, was to bring spiritual comfort and communion to one William Witter, a blind and aged fellow Baptist who had invited the three to come to his home. Witter, who could enjoy no Baptist fellow-ship in Massachusetts (for the first congregation of that per-suasion did not come into existence there until 1665), is described in an early account as a "brother in the church."[4] Though this need not imply actual membership, it does sug-gest that the Newport church was prepared to minister to those who could find no like-minded leadership near at hand. Witter, even in Massachusetts, was no closet Baptist. As early as 1646 he had been summoned before the Grand Jury in Salem "for saying that they who stayed while a child is baptized do worship the devil." Ordered to confess his error or retract, Witter did neither, thereby subjecting himself to repeated appearances before courts in Salem, Lynn, and Bos-ton. Members of the court "expressed their patience toward him, only admonishing him till they see if he continue obsti-nate."[5] But obstinate he remained, his invitation to the New-port trio being further evidence of his stubborn heart.

The broader purpose of the journey by Clarke, Crandall, and Holmes was, of course, an evangelical one: to tell of the new baptism and its import to all who would hear.[6] And indeed the word was proclaimed, converts were baptized, the elements of the Lord's Supper were served — all of this done privately in William Witter's home. On Sunday, July 20, as Clarke began to expound upon the temptations to error all around and upon "that word of promise made to those that keep the word of His patience," two constables entered the house. "With their clamorous tongues" they interrupted Clarke's discourse, "telling us that they were come with au-thority from the Magistrate to apprehend us." Clarke asked to see the authority for so rude an intrusion,[7] "whereupon they plucked forth their warrant, and one of them with a trembling hand (as conscious he might have been better employed) read it to us":

> By virtue hereof, you are required to go to the house of William Witter, and so to search from house to house for certain erroneous persons, being strangers, and them to apprehend and in safe custody to keep; and tomorrow morning by eight of the clock to bring before me.
>
> Robert Bridges[8]

The three Rhode Islanders were placed under arrest and taken to the local "Ale-house or Ordinary," Anchor Tavern, to be fed and to await their scheduled appearance before the local magistrate, Robert Bridges, early the next morning. But it was a dull Sunday afternoon in Anchor Tavern. So one of the two constables suggested to the three trespassers that if they were free (presumably, no humor intended), then all might go together to the Lynn church for evening services. Clarke replied (presumably, humor intended) that if they were free, none of this awkwardness would have happened. Yet, he said, we are at your disposal and if you want us to go to church we will go to church. Off they went, therefore, to the Puritans' meeting-house, where the resident ministers were Samuel Whiting and Thomas Cobbet. On the way, however, Clarke informed the constable that if forced to attend "your meeting, we shall declare our dissent from you both by word and gesture." Believing this to be a problem for sacred officers, not civil ones, the constable held his peace.

Upon entering the church, where services were already underway, the three visitors took off their hats, "civilly saluted," sat down, and put their hats back on again. This action was more than rude: the replacing of hats was an open declaration of disapproval of whatever was being said or done. The constable quickly snatched three hats from three irreverent heads, and "where he laid mine," wrote Clarke, "there I let it lie until their prayer, singing and preaching was over." But when all was finally over, Clarke arose to ask leave to say a few words explaining why the three had put their hats back on. While the pastor, the magistrate (for Bridges was also present), and various others argued about whether Clarke should be permitted to speak, Clarke spoke — though briefly: "... Mr. Bridges told me I [was] done ... and so commanded me silence." The three were returned to the tavern, where they were "watched over that night as thieves and robbers." In the morning, after a brief appearance before Robert Bridges in Lynn, the itinerant evangelists were sent to Boston for trial.[9]

The charge to the keeper of the Boston prison was that he take custody of "the bodies of John Clarke, Obadiah Holmes, and John Crandall and them to keep until the next County Court to be held at Boston, that they may then and there answer to such complaints as may be alleged against them."[10] This mittimus, or court order for commitment to prison, indicated essentially four complaints against the "strangers." They had offended by a) conducting a private worship service at the same time as the town's public worship; b) "offensively disturbing" the public meeting in Lynn; c) more seriously, "seducing and drawing aside [of] others after their erroneous judgment and practices"; and d) "neglecting or refusing to give in sufficient security for their appearance" at the next meeting of the county court.

After the Rhode Island Baptists had spent a week or so in Boston's prison, the day of trial came. The trial itself was so swiftly consummated that the accused hardly knew it was done. We were examined in the morning, wrote Clarke, and sentenced in the afternoon — sentenced "without producing either accuser, witness, jury, law of God or man. . . ." In the sentencing, particular emphasis was placed upon the "seducing of others" and notably upon the "re-baptizing" of others. But, insisted the three accused, they were not "re-baptizers," since the baptism which they administered was the only real baptism, infant baptism being no valid ordinance at all. This brand of apologetics only threw the Court into a paroxysm of fury.

> You affirmed that you never did re-baptize any, yet did acknowledge you did baptize such as were baptized before. And thereby [you] did necessarily deny the baptism that was before to be baptism, the Churches no Churches, and also all other ordinances and ministers — as if all were a nullity! And also [you] did in the Court deny the lawfulness of baptizing of infants; and all this tends to the dishonor of God, the despising the ordinances of God among us, the peace of the Churches, and seducing the subjects of this Commonwealth from the truth of the Gospel of Jesus Christ, and perverting the straight ways of the Lord. . . .[11]

A single infection could become a plague; the Bay authorities were out to sterilize and neutralize it now, if at all possible.

The same essential charges were levelled against all three men, all of whom fell under the clear proscription of the

1645 law against Anabaptists. The penalty which that law, with equal clarity, provided was banishment. But what sort of punishment is it to "banish" persons who already live in another jurisdiction? Obviously, some other manner of rebuke had to be meted out, whether the law made provision for it or not. Clarke, clearly the spokesman and leader of the group, was fined £20; Crandall, as a tag-along and largely silent companion, was fined only £5. But Obadiah Holmes, already under the cloud of excommunication from the church in Rehoboth, received the largest fine: £30. All the fines provided for a hard alternative: to be paid in full or else the culprit was to be "well whipped." Until the fines were paid or satisfaction otherwise received, all three were to remain in jail.

The court had spoken.[12] But John Clarke thought it only fitting that the accused also be permitted to speak. At least, asked Clarke, let us know by what law or precedent we have been found guilty. Since the relevant law provided for neither fining nor flogging, the court temporized and bickered back and forth until Governor John Endicott lost his temper, shouting that Clarke deserved death more than a fine and that he, Endicott, "would not have such trash" brought into the Bay Colony's jurisdiction. Besides, added the governor, you prey upon the weak and ignorant who are no match for your zeal and arguments, but against our own learned clergy you would never stand a chance. Aha, thought Clarke, I am being offered an opportunity to debate openly and publicly. What good fortune, now that you mention it, he started to tell John Endicott, but the latter "commanded the jailer to take us away." Back in court the next morning, however, Clarke declared that he did "readily accept" the offer of a public disputation so that he could testify to "the faith and order which I hold and practice."[13] At this point the court was unsure that any offer had been made, and if so, of what sort. The only debate, it turned out, was in court; and that was a debate over whether some Great Debate should be permitted. None ever was, and Clarke had to content himself with publishing the next year in London a statement concerning his "faith and order" — and much else besides.[14]

After another week or ten days in prison, Clarke was released (August 11, 1651) when friends paid his £20 fine. John Crandall put up bail and went home, returning later to discuss with the jailer the terms of his full release or the time when his case was to be called. Crandall left again for Newport, and a series of misunderstandings ensued in which the jailer lost some money and Crandall some credibility. So only Holmes remained in prison, adamantly refusing to pay his fine or to let others pay it for him.[15] The court's explicit alternative awaited him — to be "well whipped."

Holmes recounted his ordeal in a letter to fellow British Baptists John Spilsbury and William Kiffin "and the rest that in London stand fast in that faith, and continue to walk steadfastly in the order of the gospel which was once delivered unto the saints by Jesus Christ."[16] While still before the Boston Court in July, Holmes had apparently aroused a special antipathy in John Wilson, pastor of Boston's first church. When he heard his sentence pronounced, Holmes responded that he blessed God that he was "counted worthy to suffer for the name of Jesus, whereupon John Wilson . . . struck me before the judgment seat and cursed me saying, 'The curse of God or Jesus go with thee.'"

The amount of Holmes' fine together with the intensity of animosity he aroused (though Thomas Cobbet vigorously denied that Wilson had struck him)[17] placed this prisoner in a singular category. He felt even more singular when, after the middle of August, he languished in prison all alone, "deprived of my two loving friends." It was then, wrote Holmes, that "the Adversary stepped in, took hold on my spirit and troubled me for the space of an hour. . . ." But the spirit of the Comforter drove the Tempter away: it pleased God "to stand at my right hand." During that time when Holmes was alone, from mid-August until September 5, Tempter and Comforter wrestled for his soul. Other friends came to pay the fine, "yet I durst not accept of deliverance in such a way." On the morning appointed for his whipping, more friends appeared to offer him some wine "and other comforts, but my resolution was not to drink wine nor strong drink until my punishment were over," lest the world say that he was sustained by anything other than the spirit of God.

Then Holmes asked his friends to leave him for a time so that "I might communicate with my God, commit myself to him, and beg strength from him." But even in this final hour the Tempter had not yet surrendered. First, said Satan, think of your reputation, your birth, your breeding, your wife, children, and friends. Swiftly, the sweet answer came: "'Tis for the Lord, I must not deny Him before the sons of men." Aha, replied Satan, that is just the point: "Is it for Him and Him alone? is it not rather for thy own or some other's sake? . . . is it not pride and self in the bottom?" This, Holmes conceded, was a strong temptation indeed; therefore, "I made diligent search after the matter. . . . After a while there was even as it had been a voice from heaven in my very soul, bearing witness with my conscience, that it was not for any man's case or sake in this world, but for my Lord's case and sake and for Him alone. . . ."

Still Satan pressed on: Consider the weakness of the flesh, the strokes of the whip, the pain, the blood. . . . Holmes prayed for courage, for strength "not to shrink or yield to the strokes, or shed tears. . . ." And at length the answer came: Just as you have already surrendered your soul to Me, now surrender your body. "And so I addressed myself in as comely a manner as I could, having such a Lord and Master to serve in this business." The jailer arrived to find a prisoner utterly calm and composed, and "even cheerfulness did come upon me." Holmes was taken outside to the market place,[18] there to await the arrival of the governor. A few moments of awkward silence followed when the Governor did not appear. Finally, Magistrate Increase Nowell told the "executioner" to proceed with his task. Holmes asked permission to speak.

NOWELL: It is not now a time to speak.
HOLMES: . . . I beseech you give me leave to speak a few

words . . . seeing I am to seal what I hold with my blood, I am ready to defend it by the Word. . . .

NOWELL: This is no time for dispute.

HOLMES: I desire to give an account of the Faith and Order I hold. . . .

HENRY FLINT: Executioner, Fellow do thine office, for this fellow here would but make a long speech to delude the people.

HOLMES: That which I am to suffer for is the Word of God and testimony of Jesus Christ.

NOWELL: No! It is for your error, and going about to seduce people.

HOLMES: Not for error! In all the time of my imprisonment . . . which of all your ministers in all that time came to convince me of error? . . . And what was the reason [the public dispute] was not granted?

NOWELL: It was [Clarke's] fault that [he] went away and would not dispute.

FLINT (to Executioner): Do your office!

HOLMES (while clothes are being stripped from him): . . . I am now come to be baptized in afflictions by your hands, that so I may have further fellowship with my Lord. [I] am not ashamed of His sufferings, for by His stripes am I healed.

As the strokes began to fall, Holmes prayed once more and in truth, he later wrote, I never "had such a spiritual manifestation of God's presence." And though the executioner spat upon his hands, and laid the three-corded whip "with all his strength" thirty times across the prisoner's bare back, yet "in a manner [I] felt it not." When the whipping was finished and Holmes was untied from the post, he turned to the magistrates and said, "You have struck me as with roses."[19]

From out of the crowd of spectators, two came forward to offer their sympathy to Obadiah Holmes — John Spur and John Hazel. Both men were promptly arrested and jailed. Spur, who had only recently (July 13, 1651) been excommunicated from the church in Salem for declaring his opposition to infant baptism, noted in his own statement of the arrest that "his heart was so taken with what he saw and heard" that he could not resist going forward to Holmes as soon as he had been untied. He went over to him, said "Praised be the Lord," and walked back with him to his prison cell. That same day (September 5) the court produced two witnesses to testify to what Spur had done. Spur did not deny it; he only asked what law he had broken, what evil he had done. I would have thought, he said, that "my practice and carriage is allowed by the word of God . . . 'Be like affectioned one towards another. . . .'" However, Spur was fined forty shillings or was to be whipped himself. A friend stepped forward to pay, but Spur declined; "yet notwithstanding the Court accepted of his proffer, and bid me gone. . . ."[20]

The wrangling in John Hazel's case grew even more involved and more absurd. Hazel, a man of sixty or more years, had been a friend and neighbor of Holmes in Rehoboth and had suffered with him the anxieties and harassments that befell the Baptists there.[21] Bringing Hazel to trial the next day, September 6, the court asked if Hazel thought "that Obadiah Holmes did well or not in coming among them to baptize and administer the sacrament. . . ." Hazel responded that he presumed he was brought into Court not for what another man had done, but for what he himself might have done. What law had he, John Hazel, broken?

ENDICOTT: You took him by the hand, did you not? And spoke to him. What said you. . .?
HAZEL: I shall refer myself unto the testimonies that may or may not be brought against me.
ENDICOTT: Well, we shall find testimony enough against you. Take him to you, keeper, and we will call you forth in public. . . .

So Hazel was taken to prison for the night and returned to the court the next day. "As soon as I was in the room, the Governor read my sentence which was that I must pay forty shillings or be well whipped." Endicott then departed, leaving the remaining magistrates (Richard Bellingham, William Hibbins, and Increase Nowell) to match words and wits with the canny old Baptist.

HAZEL: I desire the privilege of an English subject . . . to wit, a jury, and to be made to appear a "Transgressor of the Law."

COURT: You have contemned authority . . . you have shown your contempt of authority in that you did take such a person by the hand as soon as he was from the post.

HAZEL: I could not do that which I did in contempt to authority, seeing he had satisfied the law to the full and was departed from the place of suffering. In the next place, what I did I did unto him as my friend. And further, if I had taken him by the hand so soon as he was loosed from the post and led him out of the town, I should not have broken any law either of God or man.

COURT: There is a law in all courts of justice . . . to punish contempt of authority. . . .

HAZEL: . . . that there is such a law I deny not . . . but what law have I broken in taking my friend by the hand when he was free and had satisfied the law?

COURT: . . . if you had shown kindness to your friend, you might have forborne in that place and done it more privately.

HAZEL: I knew not but that place was as free as any other. . . .[22]

But the sentence stood, and Hazel was returned to jail, to stay there until either the fine was paid (which Hazel refused to do) or the whipping administered, in his case only ten strokes — the amount prescribed, noted Hazel, for "common whoredom" or for an Indian found guilty of counterfeiting money. Since the fine was not paid, a whipping was scheduled for the next day, then the next, and the next. After five days of such postponements, the jailer told Hazel that he would not be whipped, that "'I might go about my business.' Then I demanded a discharge . . . he bade me go, he would discharge me." Freed, one suspects, by a thoroughly embarrassed court,

Hazel wrote his account of the episode on September 13, 1651; a few days later he died from illness and age.

Meanwhile, Obadiah Holmes had returned briefly to his prison cell, where an old friend of his "with much tenderness, like the good Samaritan, poured oil into my wounds and plastered my sores." Holmes heard that the court even tried to find out who this good Samaritan was, "but what was done I yet know not." A week after receiving his thirty lashes, Holmes wrote a letter of bitter protest to Governor Endicott, affirming his innocence and accusing the governor personally of implying that Holmes was "an evil person in life and conversation." What evidence exists for such a charge, Holmes asked. Where was the evil done and when — in Salem? in Rehoboth? in Lynn? It is even rumored that in Lynn "I baptized Goodwife Bowdish naked," but I know better than to do such a thing as that; moreover, her husband and many other witnesses who were present can testify "that she had comely garments from the crown of her head to the sole of her foot."[23] There was even a rumor of adultery: "God forbid that I should take the members of Christ and make them the members of an Harlot."[24]

Holmes concluded by challenging any or all who spread these and other untruths to "come forth before any to meet me in private or public" and not "reproach me behind my back." He closed his letter to Endicott in this fashion: "Yours still as formerly to command in all lawful things, Obadiah Holmes." In all lawful things, Governor.

But the strongest communication Endicott received came from an interested Rhode Island observer who had not been a direct party to any of these events of the summer of '51. That person was Roger Williams.[25] When Clarke was released from prison on August 11, he returned to Rhode Island where he immediately notified Roger Williams of what was going on in Boston. Writing to Endicott even before the sentence against Holmes was carried out, Williams castigated the governor for meddling as a civil magistrate "in matters of conscience and religion, as also of persecuting and hunting for any matter merely spiritual and religious." All of the old anger flooded back, as Williams recalled what Massachusetts had done to him some fifteen years before. "The Maker and Searcher of our hearts knows with what bitterness I write. . . ." The magistrate who arrogates to himself the awesome responsibility of driving out of the country every dissenter, heretic, blasphemer, or seducer may just be persecuting Christ himself.

> It is a dreadful voice from the King of Kings and Lord of Lords: "Endicott, Endicott, why huntest thou me? Why imprisonest thou me? why finest? why so bloodily whippest. . .?" Yes Sir; I beseech you, remember that it is a dangerous thing to put this to the maybe, to the venture or hazard, to the possibility.[26]

It is time to ask yourself, Williams asserted, whether in all this persecution and hunting, you do not hunt the life of your Savior "and the blood of the lamb of God." Ask yourself, John Endicott: "I have fought against several sorts of consciences; is it beyond all possibility and hazard that I have not fought against God, that I have not persecuted Jesus in some of them?"[27] If Endicott had answers for these sharp questions, no record of them survives.

Endicott was thrown on the defensive even more the next year. Letters from Holmes and Williams were, after all, private communications and still within the neighborhood, if not the family. However, with the publication in London of John Clarke's *Ill Newes from New-England* (1652), the situation radically changed. A government led by Oliver Cromwell looked askance at the persecution of a sect whose members held positions of prominence both in Cromwell's army and in Cromwell's official family. John Clarke, now in London, saw that word of the Bay Colony's behavior reached the inner circle. He was successful because regrettably, as a later governor of Massachusetts wrote, "no sect could fail of an advocate in Cromwell's court."[28] For some years the Massachusetts authorities found themselves hard pressed to defend their actions against these Baptists. When they appointed John Leverett as their colonial agent in 1655, one of his instructions read:

ILL
NEWES
FROM
NEW-ENGLAND:
OR

A Narative of *New-Englands*

PERSECUTION.

WHERIN IS DECLARED

That while old *England* is becoming new,
New-England is become Old.

Also four Proposals to the Honoured Parliament and Councel of State,
touching the way to *Propagate the Gospel of Christ* (with small
charge and great safety) both in Old *England* and New.

Also four conclusions touching the faith and order of the Gospel of
Christ out of his last Will and Testament, confirmed and justified

By JOHN CLARK Physician of Rode Island in *America*.

Revel. 2. 25. *Hold fast till I come.*
     3. 11. *Behod I come quickly.*
   22. 20. *Amen, even so come Lord Jesus.*

LONDON,

Printed by *Henry Hills* living in *Fleet-Yard* next door to the *Rose*
and *Crown,* in the year 1 6 5 2.

The title page of John Clark's *Ill Newes from New-England*

That you also humbly desire on our behalf that, seeing our
former agent is dead and we have many enemies in the world,
that all complaints made against us by one or other may take no
place in his [Cromwell's] princely breast, but be suspended from
all belief till we may have knowledge thereof and opportunity to
answer for ourselves.[29]

Apparently Leverett had some initial success in discharg-
ing this portion of his duty, for in 1656, Endicott wrote to
Cromwell expressing gratitude (and relief) that Cromwell
had received their communications through Leverett. Without such explanations as Leverett was able to provide, "we
have cause to fear, we cannot be secure from the clamors and
calumnies of some whose endeavors may be to render us
obnoxious to your pleasure."[30] Yet, royal anxieties festered.
Leverett needed still more detail on the Holmes matter; Endicott responded on June 29, 1657: "Yet I cannot for the
present answer your expectation touching Rhode Island and
Clarke and Holmes, but I have acquainted the rest of the
magistrates with your letter, who are all ready to gather up
sufficient testimony to prove what you spoke to the Protector,
and enough to satisfy (we doubt not) your opponent [John
Clarke?], if he be a lover of truth."[31]

A former Massachusetts magistrate long since returned
to England, Richard Saltonstall, also voiced his protest in
1652 or 1653. Writing to John Wilson and John Cotton, the
pastors of Boston's First Church, Saltonstall spoke of the
sadness with which he had read "of your tyranny and
persecutions in New England, as that you fine, whip and
imprison men for their consciences." (Saltonstall may have
been peculiarly sensitive to the whipping business since in
1630 he had been fined for whipping two persons illegally.)[32]
The Bay Colony, Saltonstall observed, first compels people to
go to a church they don't care for, then "when they show their
dislike thereof and witness against it . . . you stir up your
magistrates to punish them." This only produces hypocrites.
London reacts negatively to what it hears from New England,
Saltonstall reported; he had even heard public prayers "that
the Lord would give you meek and humble spirits, not to

strive so much for uniformity. . . ." He concluded with the hope that "you do not assume to yourselves infallibility of judgment, when the most learned of the Apostles confessed he knew but in part and saw but darkly as through a glass. . . ."[33]

Stung sharply by this criticism, Roger Williams' old adversary John Cotton — though in the final months of his life — responded with equal force and some sarcasm. We are not as bad as you have heard, Cotton wrote, for we do not presume to achieve a perfect uniformity and we do not pretend to infallibility. "Uniformity God never required, infallibility he never granted us." But if our laws compelling men to conform do make hypocrites, it is "yet better to be hypocrites than profane persons. Hypocrites give God part of his due — the outward man, but the profane person gives God neither outward nor inward man." We tolerate many who dissent "privately and inoffensively," Cotton declared, but we are not "so vast in our indulgence or toleration as to think the men you speak of suffered an unjust censure." Obadiah Holmes' whipping "was more voluntarily chosen by him than inflicted on him." With respect to keeping the men in prison for several weeks, a Boston jail was probably more comfortable than a Newport house. And concerning Holmes specifically, "I am sure [he] had not been so well clad for many years before."[34]

If these were the few parting shots of an old man, it fell to a younger man, Thomas Cobbet, to roll out all the guns against the "clamors and calumnies" stemming from the publication of *Ill Newes*. Cobbet, pastor of the church in Lynn where the whole affair got started, had been eyeing Baptists with keen suspicion for years. After some delay in getting it to press, Cobbet had published in 1648 *A Just Vindication of the Covenant and Church-Estate of Children of Church-Members; As also of their Right unto Baptisme*.[35] Directed against John Spilsbury among others, the book defended infant baptism to the hilt, even as it attacked "re-baptizers" to the same degree. "It is the unhappiness of our age," Cobbet wrote, "that old rotten errors are even raised out of their sepulchres, and anciently avowed truths become the ball of contention." Anabaptism is one such rotten error, and "I have not been unwilling — if I might hope to do any service to Christ — by debating, detecting, and disproving thereof. . . ." For 296 pages, Cobbet was not unwilling. When Baptists actually appeared on his doorstep in Lynn some three years later, Cobbet was ready and eager.[36] And when a copy of *Ill Newes* made its way from London to Lynn, Cobbet (with his primary treatise already written) immediately dashed off a sharp rebuttal in the "straits of four or five days time."[37]

Before receiving his copy of Clarke's "scandalous pamphlet," Cobbet was busy putting the finishing touches on *The Civil Magistrates Power in Matters of Religion*.[38] This, Cobbet correctly perceived, was the crux of the dispute between the Baptists and the Puritans, whether in London or in Boston. Baptist views on the limits of civil government, more than their views on baptism or church order or human learning or any other single doctrine, was their most distinguishing as well as their most disturbing tenet to the Puritan majority.[39] And so Cobbet intended that this treatise, even more than the one in 1648, should finish off the Baptists. In dedicating it to Oliver Cromwell, Cobbet sought to show why "civil Christian governments . . . ought in their civil and political way to restrain and punish abuses and enormities, even in matters of the Lord and of the Church."[40] *Ill Newes* simply gave Cobbet the opportunity to apply a general principle to a quite specific case, showing in the process that Clarke's "faithful and true narrative" had neither of those virtues. To his 108-page treatise on the civil magistrate, Cobbet therefore appended a 52-page "Brief Answer to a Scandalous Pamphlet called, Ill news from New-England, written by John Clark of Rhode-Island, Physitian," with "Postscript."

In *Ill Newes,* Clarke had presented a four-point testimony on behalf of Holmes, Crandall, and himself. Cobbet dealt with each point in turn. The three dissenters had begun by asserting what seemed almost beyond cavil or dispute: namely, that Jesus Christ was fully Lord and King, the Anointed One, the High Priest and Prophet, Ruler over all. Well yes, responded Cobbet, but if Christ's ruling power is understood as excluding civil rulers from "politically ratifying His orders and

THE
CIVIL MAGISTRATES
POVVER

S. W.

In matters of Religion Modestly
Debated, Impartially Stated according to the
Bounds and Grounds of Scripture, And Answer
returned to those Objections against the same
which seem to have any weight in them.

TOGETHER WITH
A Brief Answer to a certain Slanderous
Pamphlet called

Ill News from New-England; *or, A Narrative*
of New-Englands *Persecution.*
By JOHN CLARK of *Road-Iland,* Physician.

By Thomas Cobbet *Teacher of the Church at* Lynne
in New-England.

Take us the foxes, the little foxes which spoil the vines, &c. Cant. **2. 15.**
Rulers are not a terror to good works, but to the evill, &c. Rom. 13. 3.

This Treatise concerning the Christian Magistrates Power, and the exerting thereof
in, and about matters of Religion, written with much zeal and judgement by Mr.
Cobbet of *New-England,* I doe allow to be printed, as being very profitable for these
times.
Feb. 7th. 1652.

Obadiah Sedgwick.

LONDON,
Printed by *W. Wilson* for *Philemon Stephens* at the Gilded Lion
in *Paul's* Churchyard. 1653.

The title page of Thomas Cobbet's *The Civil Magistrates Power* civilly punishing such as shall disturb and contemptuously oppose the same, or as excluding the Elders of the Church as under and for Christ exercising ecclesiastically acts of rule . . . then under these fair speeches lies deceit. . . ."[41] Second, Clarke and the others had testified to the validity of baptism "of a visible believer or disciple of Christ" by immersion; but Cobbet abruptly noted that "no new light" on that matter was shed here and therefore his 1648 treatise disposed of it. Third, the testimony declared that every Christian had the duty, and therefore ought to have the liberty, "to improve that talent which the Lord has given unto him." That has a nice sound to it, Cobbet admitted: "If poison lay not underneath, it might be said there is some truth in this."[42] The poison is that such a general rule would justify even an Obadiah Holmes who, though already cast out of the church, could come to Lynn to "preach and baptize as he did." The ultimate argument, however, against this general rule that every believer develop his own gift is that even women would begin to "preach and administer the seals in a church." Further refutation was redundant.

Holmes, Clarke, and Crandall, who regarded their fourth and final point as the most crucial, devoted nearly twenty pages of *Ill Newes* to a strong defense of liberty of conscience. No servant of Christ Jesus, they wrote, has "any liberty, much less authority, from his Lord to smite his fellow servant, nor yet with outward force or arm of flesh to constrain or restrain his conscience; no, nor yet his outward man for conscience sake or worship of his God, where injury is not offered to the person, name or estate of others. . . ."[43] Cobbet, equally concerned to reply at length on this point, employed logic, scripture, and history to refute the dissenters' position. And along the way he scored some effective points: for example, Cobbet pointed to the contradiction in *Ill Newes,* which on the one hand praised Cromwell and his use of the "sword of steel" against all enemies, while on the other hand it condemned the Bay Colony's exercise of civil power in religious concerns. On Christ's parable of the wheat and the tares ("Let them grow to the harvest"), the arguments flew from both

39

sides. Cobbet contended that Christ in his exposition of the parable spoke not one whisper to suggest that he requires "Church or Commonwealth officers to let all the children of the wicked, seducers, traitors, seditious and schismatical persons, blasphemers, professed atheists, etc. [to go] unpunished."[44]

Recognizing that his primary audience was more England than New England, Cobbet innocently inquired what Britain's situation would be if this pernicious Baptist view prevailed. How could Cromwell and party "condemn and damn Episcopal Government in the Church and all their trash," or root out the Book of Common Prayer? The doctrines in *Ill Newes*, if taken seriously, he continued, would even stain "that which has been and is the glory of that religious State throughout the Reformed part of the world." No, if England (and Cromwell) will look closely, they will see "how nearly our Government here has trodden in their steps, making coercive laws against what they have forbidden by law under civil penalties — albeit the penalties possibly not in every point the same." (The last comment was as far as Cobbet was prepared to go by way of concession.) What we expect from England, he added, is not criticism but encouragement, "to go on and prosper in [our] holy zeal, to vindicate the name, truth, worship and ways of Jesus Christ from all such as would subtilely spoil us of them in whole or in part."[45]

And if Obadiah Holmes, John Spur, John Hazel, and such as that "are to be let alone unrestrained and [un]punished, both civil government and state and churches here would soon be blown up and we should become a very chaos." If the law against Anabaptists called for banishment rather than fine or lash, one must remember that banishment "is a greater punishment to an inhabitant but little or none to a stranger." True, Obadiah Holmes was severely whipped, but "possibly he had some mind to be talked of for losing his blood for that cause." Besides, Scripture provides for the use of the rod not only with children but "for the back of him that is void of understanding" (Prov. 10:13). One can only conclude, therefore, that corporal punishment of this sort is "not a mere way

40

of parental punishing of children in a family for their folly, but [of] punishing of other fools to the civil state."[46]

Thus, Obadiah Holmes, a fool for Christ, had his brief moment on the stage of history. But how quickly the lights were dimmed: no biography was ever written, no portrait ever painted or statue erected, no church or school ever bore his name. Isaac Backus in his *History* tried to rescue the reputation of Holmes for posterity, as he successfully did that of Roger Williams; but somehow it did not work. "True and impartial history," Backus wrote in 1791, "is one of the most difficult services in the world."[47]

CHAPTER 3

"The Frailty and Uncertainty of this Present Life" (1652-1682)

SHORTLY BEFORE THE WHIPPING EPISODE, OBADIAH HOLMES and his family had moved to Newport, Rhode Island, a town which John Clarke and others had formed in 1639. By 1648 the church organized by Clarke consisted of only twelve members, but in 1652 it welcomed a new influx of blood and will.[1] Among those joining the church at that time were Obadiah Holmes and John Crandall, Clarke's two companions on the fateful journey to Lynn. Joseph Torrey, who had earlier been hauled into the Plymouth Court along with Holmes, also entered the Newport church in 1652. And that same year America's first black Baptist, "Jack a colored man," was baptized and added to the church's membership roll.[2]

Almost immediately the task of pastoral leadership fell to Obadiah Holmes. For John Clarke sailed with Roger Williams for England in the fall of 1651 to obtain a secure charter for the young colony of Rhode Island and Providence Plantations. Though Williams returned in 1654, Clarke stayed on for another nine years until he was able to bring back a permanent charter that authorized "a lively experiment, that a most flourishing civil state may stand and best be maintained . . . with a full liberty in religious concernments, and that true piety rightly grounded upon gospel principles will give the best and greatest security to sovereignty. . . ."[3]

In Clarke's twelve-year absence from Newport, Holmes had the principal ministerial responsibility, though he was ably assisted by Mark Lucar (a member already in 1648), John Crandall, and Joseph Torrey.[4] None of the four lived on salaries paid by the church. First of all, the modest size of the membership made this impossible; but secondly — and more a matter of principle — a paid ministry violated the earliest Baptist practice both in England and the colonies. *A Hireling Ministry none of Christs,* Roger Williams had written in 1652, declaring that "He that makes a trade of preaching, that makes the cure of souls and the charge of men's eternal welfare a *trade,* a *maintenance*, a *living*, and that explicitly makes a covenant or bargain . . . the Son of God never sent . . . to be a laborer in his vineyard." Williams also regarded a paid ministry as singularly unproductive and notoriously insincere. They go "from Popery to Protestantism, from Protestantism to Popery, from Popery to Protestantism again! From Prelacy to Presbytery, from Presbytery many to Independency, and will [turn] again to Presbytery and Prelacy, if not to Popery . . . rather than lose (as they say) the Liberty of Preaching!" Williams recognized that the weight both of history and of human nature were against him, but he believed the future was for him: "If all the princes, states, parliaments and armies in the world should join their heads and hearts and arms and shoulder to support" a hired ministry, that babel will still sink "as a millstone . . . into the deeps forever."[5]

From the perspective of seventeenth-century Baptists, a paid ministry was synonymous with a state-controlled and state-subsidized ministry. And while the radical rejection of all compensation for ministerial labors was later abandoned by the Baptists (to be taken up by the Quakers), the profound concern about a state-paid clergy remained. As Isaac Backus wrote to George Washington in 1790, "religious ministers when supported by force are the most dangerous men on earth. . . ."[6] So John Clarke described himself on the title-page of *Ill Newes* as a "physician of Rhode Island." And so Obadiah Holmes, whether in Salem, Rehoboth or Newport, continued to labor as craftsman or artisan or farmer that he not be guilty of making a trade out of preaching.

Together with three former associates from Rehoboth (Edward Smith, James Mann, and William Devel), Holmes purchased the Sachuset Farm in Newport (now Middletown), Rhode Island in or near 1650. On March 1, 1658, Holmes bought a sizable portion of this farm, about one hundred acres, for his exclusive use and that of his family. This deed, in specifying which portion of Holmes' land was to be used for grazing cattle, which for orchard, garden, feed crops and the like, offers some insight into Obadiah Holmes' life as a farmer.[7] But he also worked as a weaver, probably making his own wool cloth from the many sheep that he kept on the farm. He pursued his craft as weaver at least into the 1670s and perhaps to the very end of life.[8]

In the 1650s the still young Newport church, now deprived of its first pastor's direct leadership, found itself surrounded by a medley of theological and ecclesiastical options. Cotton Mather was right: seventeenth-century Rhode Island bubbled with new sects, new visions, new and frightening lifestyles. And America's new-born Baptists were not yet sure which was a true light and which a false fire. Nor were they certain how far they should go in tolerating differences in opinion or practice within their own fellowship. Toleration in the colony, yes; but for those who voluntarily covenanted with one another to walk together in a new life — for those, how much diversity was permitted, how much idiosyncrasy allowed? That abstract question soon emerged as a concrete issue: it concerned the "laying on of hands."

Traditionally in Baptist churches, or elsewhere among Christian groups, the ceremonial placing of hands (by the clergy or elders) on the head of a younger brother constituted the means by which he was set aside for the ministry (as deacon, presbyter, or bishop in historic Christianity). But since priesthood was now conceived of as universal among Protestants, emphatically so among early Baptists, should not all members, brothers and sisters alike, be set apart for what Holmes later called the "feeding ministry in the church"?[9] Thus the question for debate was formulated in this way: after baptism of the believer, but before admitting him or her to the Lord's Supper, may one, *must* one formally lay hands upon every new member? As early as 1652, Samuel Hubbard

44

and his wife, and possibly other members of the church, had the hands of an elder formally placed upon their heads. For some years, then, the practice was clearly optional, being no bar to fellowship whether one participated in that additional ceremony or not. One *may* lay hands upon the new member; by 1656, however, some had turned "may" into "must," and Six-Principle Baptists were the result.

The six principles were drawn from Hebrews 6:1, 2: "Therefore, leaving the principles of the doctrine of Christ, let us go on unto perfection; not laying again the foundation of [1] repentance from dead works, and of [2] faith toward God, of the [3] doctrine of baptisms, and of [4] laying on of hands, and of the [5] resurrection of the dead, and of [6] eternal judgment."[10]

The church in Providence, rent by the issue as early as 1652, continued for over a century to be troubled by partisans for and against the laying on of hands.[11] The Newport Church suffered so severe a schism in 1656 that its very survival was threatened. Of a church membership of fewer than fifty, some twenty-one members firmly embraced that sixth principle and so withdrew from the church led by Holmes, Lucar, Torrey, and Crandall to launch Newport's second Baptist church. (Newport was the only town in seventeenth-century America to have two Baptist church bodies; and fifteen years later it would have a third!) While superficially the quarrel concerned only a minor matter of church order, a deeper theological orientation was at stake. Those of the Six-Principle persuasion pulled away from Calvinism back toward the Arminianism of England's earliest Baptists. These General Baptists, as distinguished from Particular Baptists, affirmed that Christ died for all rather than for a "particular" group of God's elect. Clarke and Holmes remained in the Calvinist tradition of the Spilsbury-Kiffin church in London, as well as in the Calvinist tradition of Puritanism generally.[12]

Late in the next year (1657), Holmes and a fellow Baptist, Samuel Hubbard, journeyed to Long Island to preach among the Calvinist Dutch on Long Island (Gravesend, Jamaica, Flushing, Hampstead). That mission, which lasted six weeks (October 1–November 15), probably helped generate the subsequent interest within Obadiah Holmes' own family in the fortunes of New York and New Jersey, to which several of his children migrated.[13] Back in Newport in 1658, Holmes opposed the marriage of two young people who had already lived together and produced a child without benefit of clergy. After Edward Richmond and Abigail Davis had each pleaded guilty to living in sin (and each had paid a fine of forty shillings), the two petitioned Rhode Island's General Court "to declare themselves condescending to the two parties' marriage together," offering as their reason for the petition a "preventing of the like temptation." The court was receptive, although they noted that twice before when the couple had tried to get married, Obadiah Holmes "forbade it, though he showed no reason nor has according to law proceeded in the matter." Having rendered its judgment in levying the fines, the court then manifested its mercy: Edward and Abigail "are married before and in the presence of this Court legally."[14]

From Holmes' own Testimony (see Part II, Section F) it is apparent that much of his ministry was carried on apart from the formal Sunday worship. And some of it, as noted, was apart from Newport. Not only did he journey at least once to Long Island, but he dared even to venture back into Massachusetts. Such could not have been an easy decision, for Roger Williams himself, despite his growing prestige abroad and powerful friends at home, found his personal security ever endangered in the Bay Colony. In letters written to the General Court of Massachusetts in 1655 and again in 1656, Williams sought written assurance that he would be neither seized nor harassed "in taking ship and landing in your ports."[15] All Williams wanted to do was travel in a straight line to Boston, board his ship and depart as soon as possible; but even that was not safe for one who had been banished.

What Obadiah Holmes wanted to do was much riskier than that: he wished to minister, to comfort, to baptize, to evangelize for more churches "of the gospel order." In 1668

46

and probably before, he counseled Baptists in Boston who had come together under the leadership of Thomas Goold to form a church. Of the seven original members of this, Boston's first Baptist church, three "were persons whom God . . . brought out of Old England, who had walked with the Baptized Churches there."[16] At least one of those three was from William Kiffin's church in London. Another three — Goold himself, John Farnum, and Thomas Osburne — were, like Holmes, former members of Congregational churches in New England and therefore were, also like Holmes, capable of arousing the special ire of the civil and ecclesiastical authorities in Massachusetts.

In October of 1668, Holmes personally visited the besieged Boston group, whose pastor (Goold) had been imprisoned along with two other members of the tiny congregation. During this pastorless interim, already of more than three months' duration, the remnant kept alive its faith and its hope by meeting each Sunday in Goold's home in nearby Charlestown. As in Lynn, the Charlestown constables charged with "the preventing of schismatical meetings on the Sabbath Day . . . did repair unto the house of Thomas Goold," there to find among the small group of worshippers one "Obadiah Holmes of Rhode Island (as he said his name was)." What happened beyond the breaking up of this "schismatical meeting" is not known. Further punitive action was probably forestalled by a petition presented the following month to the Bay Colony authorities by sixty-five prominent (i.e., non-Baptist) citizens. This remarkable address to the court asked that mercy be shown the three imprisoned Baptists (Goold, Farnum, and William Turner) "separated from their wives and children, disabled to govern or to provide for their families." Noting that they "neither approve of their judgment or practice," the petitioners nonetheless thought mercy appropriate "considering that the men are reputed godly and of a blameless conversation; and the things for which they seem to suffer seem not to be moral, unquestioned, scandalous evils, but matters of religion and conscience: not in things fundamental, plain, clear — but circumstantial, more dark

47

and doubtful, wherein the saints are wont to differ and to forbear one another in love, . . ."[17] The immediate response displayed neither forbearance nor love: the petitioners were reprimanded and fined for their plea.

But slowly sentiment was altering. Goold himself, a wagonmaker and farmer, enjoyed a close relationship with many of the Winthrop family, especially John Winthrop, Jr. This younger Winthrop, who served as governor of Connecticut from 1657 to 1675 (except for one year as lieutenant governor) stood out as a Puritan who, in Roger Williams' words, has "always been noted for tenderness toward men's souls." Goold, who rented land from the Winthrops in Charlestown from the 1650s on, is casually referred to as "Mr. Winthrop's farmer" a decade later.[18] Obadiah Holmes also enjoyed a warm relationship with John Winthrop, Jr., exchanging letters with him as early as 1660. He signed his letters to Winthrop, "your friend," sent the greetings of his wife, "who is always glad when we hear from you," and invited Winthrop to "come to our Island" and stay with them — all these incidental courtesies suggested that, at least in a few circles, the sharp and sometimes cruel divisions between establishment and dissent were softening.[19]

A more public softening occurred in April 1668, when the Bay authorities permitted the public disputation which John Clarke had vainly sought seventeen years before.[20] Such a debate and fair show of tolerance might seem more expedient now in view of old England's growing restlessness about New England's apparently growing intolerance, an intolerance tragically manifested against the Quakers. A certain restlessness also appeared among the churches of the Standing Order themselves, as controversy heightened on questions of church admission and eligibility for baptism.[21] So, on April 14 and 15, the debate took place, with ten Baptist lay preachers (John Crandall among them) on one side and a like body of Congregational clergy and civil officers (Thomas Cobbet among them) on the other. Each saw the other in terms of its most frightening potential. The Baptists, if victorious, would overthrow all church order, laws, families, covenants, and so forth, until the whole country consisted of nothing but Ranters, Seekers, lawbreakers, and — as Emerson later wrote — every man his own sect. The Congregationalists, if victorious, would mix law and gospel hopelessly, would advocate conversion by heredity, salvation by works, and would lead the whole church of Jesus Christ back to the old "whore of Babylon." Not surprisingly, no winner was declared; the most remarkable fact was that a debate could be held at all.[22]

Despite the debate, Goold, Turner, and Farnum (as noted above) were placed in Boston's prison in the summer of 1668. After three months' incarceration, the three wrote a restrained, lightly ironic, but altogether respectful letter to the court (October 14, 1668), reminding the court that they were still in bonds and saying: "We should be glad, if it might be thought to stand with the honor and safety of the country and the present government thereof, to be now at liberty." Six months later, the court, apparently deciding that the country could survive only a brief spurt of outlaw freedom, gave Goold and Turner three days' leave from prison to attend to personal business. (Farnum, by recanting, had been released earlier.) Goold and Turner fled to Noddles Island in Boston harbor — just far enough away to be out of the town's jurisdiction — where for five years Goold maintained a Baptist fellowship in exile.[23] In 1674, Goold returned to the Boston-Charlestown area, where Baptists continued to meet in private homes until 1679, when they thought it safe to build a meeting house.[24] Yet, for another two years civil officers continued to harass, to make arrests, and even at one point to nail shut the doors of the newly built church. In all of this long tribulation, messages, messengers, and "prison epistles" flowed back and forth between the "church of Christ" in Newport and the one in Boston. When Boston Baptists saw nothing but black clouds gathering overhead, they wrote to their Newport brothers and sisters, imploring that "we may be remembered in your prayers to our Heavenly Father who can do abundantly above what we can ask or think. . . ."[25]

But if Baptists fared badly in Massachusetts, Quakers fared far worse. The hanging of Newport's Mary Dyer on May

21, 1660 further dramatized the extreme fear manifested when her two younger companions (William Robinson and Marmaduke Stephenson) had been sent to the gallows the previous October. From Boston's point of view, everything possible had been done to warn the Quakers away: fines, whips, long months in cold prison cells, ears cut off. And still they came, Rufus Jones wrote, "just as though they were wanted" to look "your bloody laws in the face."[26] Obadiah Holmes' former glass-house partner and neighbor in Salem, Lawrence Southwick, became a Quaker in 1657, was arrested and imprisoned along with his wife Cassandra in 1658, and in 1659 was banished from Salem and from Massachusetts. Lawrence and Cassandra Southwick made their way to Sylvester Island, near the eastern end of Long Island, where in November 1660 Lawrence died.[27] When Charles II came to the throne in that same year, he urged New England to suspend its laws — as England had done — that involved corporal punishment or death for religious dissent. In a long and defensive letter to the king, Endicott explained what New England's "errand into the wilderness" was all about and why it was impossible to endure those "open and capital blasphemers, open seducers from the glorious Trinity, the Lord Jesus Christ . . . the blessed gospel, open enemies to the government. . . ."[28] Then, a few years later, respected Congregational ministers in London added their pressure for a greater toleration of dissenters, whether they be Quakers, Baptists or Anglicans.

> We only make it our hearty request to you, that you would trust God with His truths and ways so far as to suspend all vigorous proceedings in corporal restraints or punishments on persons that dissent from you, and practice the principles of their dissent without danger or disturbance to the civil peace of the place.[29]

Cotton Mather acknowledged that "this excellent letter" did not have "immediately all the effect it should have had,"[30] but the excesses of the 1650s and the early 1660s had begun to wane by the end of the latter decade.

Crises of a different nature confronted Obadiah Holmes back in Newport. Beginning in 1665 his church found itself again threatened by internal discord and tension. The previous issue had concerned the sixth principle; now it involved the seventh day. Early that year Stephen Mumford had arrived in Newport from the Bell Lane Seventh-Day Baptist Church in London. Almost immediately he began to woo some members of the Newport Church, arguing that the ancient commandment to the Hebrews to keep the Sabbath holy meant precisely that. The first day of the week, established as the "Christian Sabbath," did not alter God's original command : the true Sabbath remained Saturday. Tacey Hubbard (wife of Samuel) "took up keeping of the Lord's holy seventh day Sabbath" on March 10, 1665; her husband was convinced three weeks later, one daughter in 1666, and two other daughters together with a son-in-law (Joseph Clarke, nephew of John Clarke) early in 1667. Soon others announced for the sabbatarian position. So swiftly did the novel sentiment appear to spread that Obadiah Holmes feared the whole church would be swept from the main current of Christianity into this diversionary stream. Probably he spoke with unusual asperity against the sabbatarians in 1667 (we know that he did so in 1671), and perhaps for this uncharitableness he was rebuked by John Clarke, now back from London. The precise sequence of events in the early years of the controversy is not known. But it is known that Holmes, feeling in some manner rebuffed or wronged, withdrew from active leadership in the church from 1667 to 1671. When he resumed his normal role in 1671, it was apparently on his terms, for events involving the sabbatarians moved quickly to a climax.

One letter from the early phase of the dispute indicates that Holmes was indeed the central figure of the opposition. Samuel Hubbard maintained correspondence with English Seventh-Day Baptists, and one of his correspondents, Thomas Trenicke, replied as follows (July 13, 1668):

> I hoped I should never have seen the day in which such fruit should be found among you, so full of gall and wormwood, as your letter seems in one part of it to intimate, in a difference betwixt you and my dear brother Holmes, whose faithfulness for Christ

51

and His truth has been so long [proved] among you many ways. The [breach] among you, I understand, is between Brother Holmes and the congregation. But having received but from one hand, I durst not assume to give judgment in the matter absolutely.[31]

The difference lay between Holmes and a *portion* of the congregation, but it was a significant and vocal portion which did not rest until schism struck again.

Samuel Hubbard (1610-1692?) had emigrated to Salem in 1633, then moved into Connecticut a few years later, and in 1648 came to Newport, where John Clarke baptized him and his wife Tacey on the third of November. Hubbard, a carpenter and a farmer, had bought twenty-five acres of farmland close to Holmes' land, and when Clarke, Holmes, and Crandall were arrested in 1651 had visited the three in Boston's prison. The year the Hubbards "took up keeping" of the Seventh Day (1665) John Crandall also became a sabbatarian, presumably under their influence; later that year Crandall moved to Westerly, Rhode Island, where a considerable portion of the Hubbard progeny had settled.[32] Besides the Hubbards, the other major figure in the Newport church's struggle was William Hiscox (1638-1704), almost a generation younger than Hubbard and thus the one destined to give years of significant leadership to what was soon to become Newport's *third* Baptist church body.

The six years between Tacey Hubbard's first apprehension of her Christian duty in 1665 and the final separation at the end of 1671 were years of painful decision and almost daily discomfort. From the sabbatarian side, the questions were these: how much proselytizing of others within the church was appropriate? could one still take communion with non-sabbatarians? how much loyalty did the Hubbard family, for example, owe to the church of Clarke and Holmes? how should one behave toward those who became sabbatarians and then changed their minds? This last question pressed acutely upon Hubbard and Hiscox when at one point four out of eleven Seventh-Day observers in the church became apostates "and turned back to full communion with the church — and not only so but prate against this holy truth." Hubbard added: "It is a very hard exercise to us, poor weak ones, to lose four so suddenly. . . ."[33] It might be possible to continue to commune with persons such as Clarke or Lucar or Torrey, but could one commune with apostates? How could one forget the apostle's command not to take communion when differences among the saints went unreconciled? Hubbard and the others, therefore, sought advice, from Providence and Boston as well as from London.[34] On the one hand, what did Christian charity propose? But on the other hand, what did Christian conscience demand? Hubbard indicated in 1669 that it was getting harder and harder for him to stay within the Newport church since the preachers talked as though the Ten Commandments were all "nailed to the cross and done away — but renewed again some of them! I am sure that can't be. . . . Oh! methinks for many reasons I could leave them quite. . . ."[35]

In April 1668, one week before the "Great Debate," Hubbard went to Boston to consult with the brothers and sisters there. Three years later Thomas Goold traveled to Newport to consult, pray, and advise, urging the sabbatarians to stay within the church "and get along as well as they could."[36] Hubbard even wrote to his own children in Westerly, asking what they would advise. On behalf of all the "children," Joseph Clarke wrote a tender and affectionate response (August 8, 1671), saying that they hardly knew what course to propose, except that there be patience and no hasty action. But if a separation had to come, the children made only two requests: 1) see that "the moving cause is only and purely in love unto the law of God"; and 2) "manage it with all humility, patience and meekness. . . ." Know, however, that through whatever may come "we remain your dutiful children."[37]

What did come could not always be characterized, on either side, as humble, patient, and meek. From the point of view of Holmes and other opponents of the sabbatarians, the central questions were these: how can one be justified in mixing the old law with the new gospel? how can one still be of the church if he refuses to commune with the church? and how much does a special attachment to the ancient sabbath become a stumbling block for those who would receive a gracious gospel? In 1671, Holmes himself became the catalyst in precipitating the final showdown. Some time that year, after Holmes had returned to his pastoral position within the church, he delivered a sermon that stuck like a bone in the throat of the sabbatarians. Hubbard summarized the offensive portion:

> Woe to the world because of offenses; it must needs be that offenses must come, but woe to them by whom they do come. It were better that a millstone were hanged about his neck and cast into the sea than that one of these little ones that believe in me should be offended [Matt. 18:6].... These offenses are not only in the world, but in the churches. And to be plain, they are such offenses as these: viz., for persons to leave Christ and [go] to Moses in the observation of days, seasons and such like.[38]

Then, as Hubbard recounts the events, John Clarke preached on the same text but in a manner more ambiguous and therefore more satisfactory to "the auditory" — so much so that Holmes was disturbed, "went out and came in no more that forenoon." That Sunday afternoon, however, Holmes returned to defend his application of the text from Matthew.

HISCOX: My question is to you, Brother Holmes, to desire you to declare who it is of this church that have left Christ and are gone to Moses....

HOLMES: If I have been faithful in the discharge of my duty and if the word did reach you, and your conscience does accuse you, do you make the application.

HISCOX: If that be all the answer you'll give, 'tis no matter. For 'tis well known who you intended, but — through grace — we have not left our Lord Jesus Christ.... Let it be taken notice of by all this day that the only difference between you and us is this. We plead for the Ten Commandments to be a rule of good living and to be obeyed [even] in gospel times. You deny them, and say they were never given to be a rule of the Gentiles before or after faith.

At this juncture Joseph Torrey tried to pour oil upon the warming waters, but Hiscox was not interested in being calmed. He replied in effect that he did not start this fight but would do his very best to finish it. So the congregation determined to set aside the next regular Thursday evening meeting of the church for a continuation of the discussion rapidly turning into a disputation. At that meeting Hiscox was asked why he and the others (now only four: Samuel and Tacey Hubbard, Rachel Hubbard Langworthy, and Roger Baster) had refused for years to take communion with the rest of the church. Hiscox reviewed the conscientious scruples of his small group concerning the Sabbath and especially the impropriety of joining in communion with apostates. Then:

HISCOX: But further, my trouble is much heightened by Brother Holmes' preaching. For if we be such persons that better a millstone were hanged about our necks, etc., it ain't likely that the Lord should smell a sweet savor in our fellowship together.

CLARKE: Brother Holmes did not name you or any other, but spoke in a general way.

HISCOX: Who is it that could be intended . . . ?

HOLMES: To be plain with you, I did intend Brother Hiscox and such as he is.

HISCOX: You have done well to own the truth, for none that heard you could judge you intended any other. . . . If it be as Brother Holmes has said, that we have no more conscience than dogs, it ain't likely that our fellowship should be any ways to our comfort and God's glory.

HOLMES: Who did say so?

HISCOX: You said so, at Brother Slocum's house.[39]

HOLMES: Take notice of this, brethren. . . . I must be plain for I do judge that you have not conscience toward God in the matter of the Sabbath; for if you had, you could not have walked so long with the church as you have done.

MARK LUCAR (with grief): The wringing of the nose causes blood.

John Clarke then took up the discussion with Hiscox, returning to the question of the church's communion and the sabbatarians' continued absence from it. Joseph Torrey thought that the congregation ought to hear from someone besides Hiscox, and after much discussion Tacey Hubbard was allowed to summarize the reasons for their not taking communion with the rest of the church: 1) the apostacy of Nicholas Wild and his wife, along with John Salmon and his wife, those four still being in the church and in its good standing; 2) "that speech of Brother Holmes"; and 3) "the dismal laying aside of the ten precepts, with the leading brethren denying of them. . . ." At this point the Thursday evening meeting was adjourned because word was received of the death of Joseph Torrey's son.

At a subsequent Thursday evening meeting (no date given, but late in 1671), discussion resumed and tempers quickly rose: "Mr. Torrey was discoursing with Mr. Hiscox with warmth. . . ."

HISCOX: What do you think? — to juggle me out of my conscience?

TORREY: If I am become a juggler, then it is time for me to leave of this matter.

HISCOX: Pray, Brother Torrey, don't be offended at it. For they were not suitable words, and I am troubled that I said so to you. I pray, pass them by.

(Torrey indicates his forgiveness, but the contest of wills continues.)

TORREY: Do you take notice of this: that though the church has endeavored to remove your scruples, yet you remain obstinate. You stand upon your peril.

HISCOX: Pray, Brother Torrey, don't threaten so. You may do what you please; your threatening words don't affright me.

(John Clarke again attempts to conciliate, suggesting that perhaps he does not altogether deny the force of the ancient laws.)

HISCOX: Pray, Brother Clarke, speak plainly to things and don't go round about the matter and leave us in the dark all the while.

CLARKE: I can't speak more plainly than I have done.

TORREY: Brother Clarke, speak plain and say they [the old laws] are done away.

(Soon this meeting adjourns, to reconvene a few days later.)

HISCOX: . . . it is a sad thing and offensive to good in other colonies to hear that the elders of this church should deny the Ten Words to be a rule in gospel times. It is a stink in their nostrils.

LUCAR (heatedly): If there be any stink, it is you that have made it.

HISCOX: No, 'tis you, the leaders of the congregation, being Yea and Nay in this matter, that is so bad a savor.

(After still more debate and "too much heat of spirit," Obadiah Holmes challenges William Hiscox to prove that his position and only his position is the correct one.)

HOLMES: We are off the subject. We should put Brother Hiscox on it to prove his Seventh Day practice, or else fall under.

HISCOX: Brother Holmes, you are not right there. You shan't slip your neck out of the collar so. For the grounds of our difference is that you and others deny God's law.

HOLMES: You are deluded and ought to be made sensible of it.

HISCOX: You have said more than this before now, as that we had denied Christ and had not conscience toward God in these matters.

HOLMES: I again say I do judge that you have [denied] and still do deny Christ, and that you have not conscience in it. . . .

TORREY: I judge that when the church has endeavored to convince them, if they remained refractory, then the church should wait awhile and after that to declare such to be none of them.

57

HISCOX: What? Must we be forced to walk by your legs and see by your eyes? You may do what you please in that matter.

As more meetings were held, the two sides grew farther apart, until "everything appeared dark as though there was no likelihood of accommodation to be one church." Though some efforts at compromise were tentatively explored, positions had solidified beyond rescue. In the final confrontation, Holmes and Hiscox faced each other again.

HOLMES: I have something of weight on my heart to declare unto the church. 1) Brother Hiscox's slandering the leading brethren in saying they deny the law. 2) His charging those four persons as apostates. In my judgment the church ought to make Brother Hiscox see his evil in charging them so highly, or else the church ought to look at them as such and declare against them. 3) It is reported that Brother Hiscox did work one First Day 'til meeting time, and then came and stood up in church to speak and to pray. 4) He has broken bread [observed the Lord's Supper] on the Seventh Day of the week. 5) He, in so doing, held communion with such as are not owned by the church. These five things are matters of great grief to me; therefore, I call upon the church to deal with Mr. Hiscox for them as great evils.

HISCOX: If you have done, Brother Holmes, I shall give you our answer to these things. For I am glad that I have now a time to speak to them, for I have heard that you and some others have spoken of such things abroad — but not to me. 1) If I have slandered the leading brethren in saying they have denied the law or the Ten Words to be a rule unto us Gentiles . . . I have said and I do say so still. And if Brother Holmes or any other do deny it, their last sin could be as bad as their first, having said it publicly and privately. Should you deny it, it would be only adding sin to sin. 2) As for my calling those four persons apostates, we can look upon them no better, for what is apostacy but the denial in a back way of that which persons once professed to be the mind and will of God? Would not you count us such if we should deny water baptism and turn our backs upon it and plead for a baptism of the Spirit only — as too, too many do at this day?

TORREY: If Apostacy be to deny that which persons once professed, then most of this church are apostates.

HISCOX: Look you to that, if you have done anything in the name of the Lord and have forsook it, whether you have need to repent of it. 3) Brother Holmes, it is grossly false, for I never in all my life came from my work to speak and pray in the church, but once. And that was many years ago and that was upon a more than ordinary occasion when Brother Clarke was sick. I cannot but wonder at you, Brother Holmes, of whom I heard before I saw your face that you could as freely weave a yard or two of cloth of a First Day, before meeting, as at any other time.

HOLMES: Did you ever see me do it?

HISCOX: No, but I have seen you come to meeting on a First Day with your leather apron on, as if you came from your work, which makes me think it might be true. Especially hearing you ofttimes say you had no Sabbath but Christ.

Hiscox never made it to points 4) and 5): ". . . there was so much disorder in the meeting that the other things were not spoke to." Joseph Torrey had the last word: namely, that he thought the church had spent enough of its time with Brother Hiscox and the others. Dialogue had turned into a wrangle and theological exploration into a shouting match.

On December 7, 1671, the final separation took place. However, the schism consisted of only five persons: Hiscox, the three Hubbards, and the silent Roger Baster. Yet, from so modest a base a new denomination was born, making its way slowly from Newport, Westerly, and New London (Connecticut) across a continent not yet known or explored.[40]

Still another ecclesiastical crisis shook the church of Clarke and Holmes in the 1670s. This new trauma, in which

Holmes was not as centrally involved as in the preceding one, concerned that pestilent and unnerving sect called Quakers. During that decade Rhode Island saw a dramatic increase both in the number of Friends and in their influence. Having been convincingly dissuaded from lodging elsewhere in New England, Quakers settled in significant numbers in and around Newport; they also proselytized with significant success. In 1672 a Newport Quaker, Nicholas Easton, was even elected governor of the colony. Not only was he re-elected the following year, but his deputy governor was none other than Clarke's old adversary, William Coddington, now also a Quaker. Quaker missionaries from abroad had "worked the territory" around Newport with excellent results, aided further by the visit of the movement's founder, George Fox, to the town in 1672.⁴¹ Already nervous from watching this sudden swell of Quakerism all around them, the Newport congregation shuddered to find the virulent heresy in their very midst. The fever first appeared in the person and household of Giles Slocum.

When the church learned that dangerous principles had penetrated their own fellowship, that body made every earnest effort to counsel, guide, convince, and reprove with love. No civil action, of course, was deemed appropriate or possible. But the church's discipline among early Baptists was real, it was careful, and it was democratic. The faithful marshaled their biblical arguments, offered their fervent prayers, and repeatedly met together — as with the sabbatarians — to comfort and if possible correct their erring fellows. Indeed, when one realizes the enormous amount of labor and love that went into cases such as this, the notion of "church discipline" takes on a profounder significance. The Slocum family's fever reached its climax in 1673, with John Clarke, Mark Lucar, and Joseph Torrey doing all in their power to rectify views that challenged or altogether voided the doctrine of Christ's divinity. But the fever did not pass. On October 16, 1673, therefore, Giles Slocum and his wife, their son, daughter, and son-in-law were excommunicated "for embracing the soul undoing error that the man Christ Jesus was not in heaven nor earth nor anywhere — that his body was entirely lost." These five, thus cut off from the Baptists, "fell in with the sad principles of Quakerism. . . ."[42]

Clarke, Lucar, and Torrey signed the order of excommunication; where was the signature of Obadiah Holmes? He could have merely been traveling again — to Massachusetts or Long Island; but it is unlikely that he would have been absent throughout the whole time of admonition and reproof. It is more probable that he deliberately excluded himself from the church's formal action on the grounds of personal friendship, for Hiscox had noted Holmes' presence in the Slocum home. It could also be that, having been so central a figure in the 1671 schism, he was simply not yet ready for another church fight. As he wrote in his Testimony in 1675, if any member should stumble or fall, "be faithful, but not too vigorous. . . . God is merciful and may raise them up again; if they repent, forgive them."[43]

In the midst of his activities as churchman, husband, father, farmer, and weaver, Obadiah Holmes also discharged many civic duties in a still young and vulnerable community. Accounted a freeman in 1655, Holmes served as a juror that year and frequently in succeeding years. In 1656 and again in 1658 he was named a commissioner, a duty involving taking testimony for the courts, administering oaths, witnessing legal transactions, and sometimes rendering judgments in "small claims" civil cases. In 1662, Holmes, along with Mark Lucar, witnessed the sale of land by an Indian chief to Roger Williams and others, and in 1667 he acted as surety for one of his fellow citizens. Of course, many of the ordinary and routine tasks of the citizen left no record behind, but enough has survived to demonstrate that Holmes kept active in this realm as well.[44]

In the mid-1670s, however, his level of activity began to decline. When — at the end of 1675 — Holmes sat down to compose his Testimony, death was much on his mind. For the next twelve months death was also much on the mind of his church and of all New England. In a single year, 1676, the Newport church lost Joseph Torrey, John Clarke, and Mark

Lucar; only Obadiah Holmes remained to carry on a pastoral leadership. Death stalked throughout all New England during 1675-1676, when colonial America's bloodiest war broke out. King Philip's War, as it came to be called, began in June 1675, when an Indian attack on Swansea, Massachusetts left nine whites dead. Other tribes soon joined with the Wampanoags, the first to go on the offensive, and in rapid succession many Massachusetts towns suffered the full effect of long-mounting Indian resentment: Brookfield, Lancaster, Deerfield, Northfield, Hadley, and others. When in the fall of 1675 the Wampanoags made an alliance with the Narragansetts, Rhode Island became acutely vulnerable — the mainland much more than the Island of Aquidneck. Warwick was utterly destroyed on March 17, 1676, and two weeks later most of the homes in Providence went up in flames. The whole of Aquidneck became a refugee center, as to some degree it had been three months earlier following the "Great Swamp Fight," when wounded soldiers poured into Newport for treatment and recuperation. (Even as early as the summer of 1675 some families fled to Newport. Samuel Hubbard noted in his Journal: "My daughter [Ruth] Burdick and her eight children and their husbands came to this island [from Westerly] for fear of the wars July, 1675.")[45]

After the havoc in Warwick and Providence, Newport found itself overwhelmed with the homeless, hungry, wounded, and orphaned. The town council allotted some of its common lands to be fenced and farmed by its temporary guests, thereby helping to feed those without means of support or survival. And in April 1676 the Rhode Island General Assembly appointed fifteen of its "most judicious inhabitants" from throughout the colony to advise that body "in these troublesome times and straits." Obadiah Holmes was one of those fifteen, as was John Clarke, who was appointed very shortly before his death on April 20.[46] At the time of the General Assembly's action, all of "mainland" Rhode Island from Providence to Point Judith had been evacuated. On August 12, 1676, Philip, "king" of the Wampanoags, was slain and the war soon ended, but not before half of the towns in

New England had been hit and a dozen or more entirely devastated.[47]

At the end of 1679, the Newport church, now under the guidance of Obadiah Holmes alone, wrote to the still suffering Baptist fellowship in Boston. That church's warm response, expressing gratitude for "the working of your affections towards us, bearing us on your hearts, making mention of us in your prayers," revealed again how strict congregational autonomy did not preclude a close and comforting community among the beleaguered Baptists. Newporters had asked "how it fared" with the Boston church in their ongoing legal difficulties. In reply, the Bostonians reported that John Russell, their pastor, was still free but "several of our brethren and sisters" had been summoned to court, where they met "with many hard and censorious speeches, and several of them were fined 20 shillings and court charges." At the moment, however, no one was in prison; moreover, rumors had begun to circulate that some degree of toleration might be on its way. Those rumors proved true.

Early in 1682 the Massachusetts Court, still on the defensive vis-à-vis the King, explained that formerly they had made "some laws to prevent the violent and impetuous intrusions of the Quakers at their first coming into these parts"; but these laws "for diverse years have been suspended . . . and, as for the Anabaptists, they are now subject to no other penal statutes than those of the Congregational way."[49] So Obadiah Holmes lived just long enough to see Boston's long arm of persecution shortened; the nails were pulled from the church doors, and Baptists openly worshipped at the corner of Salem and Stillman streets. And many Quakers lived long enough to see, by 1682, a whole new colony established by William Penn, a colony of unbelievable expanse offering even more unbelievable guarantees for liberty of conscience.

On April 9, 1681, "being by daily intimations put in mind of the frailty and uncertainty of this present life," Obadiah Holmes wrote his will. At the same time he made out a deed of sale for the family farm to be passed on to his son Jonathan.

And with the farm of about one hundred acres went all its "dwellings, houses, outhouses, barns" and much livestock.[50] On October 15, 1682, Holmes died. He was buried on that Middletown farm (in the "middle" between the older communities of Newport and Portsmouth), about one-half mile west of the Sakonnet River, which flows toward the open sea. In a tiny family cemetery, a modest tablet marks his grave.

LAST WILL & TESTIMONY

General Introduction

THE LITERARY REMAINS OF OBADIAH HOLMES ARE REVEALING — BUT
certainly not extensive. No multivolume edition of his "collected
works" will ever be possible; no bibliography of published writings
need ever be written. Holmes appeared in print only once in his
lifetime, and then not under his own name. His long letter to
William Kiffin and John Spilsbury, along with his shorter letter to
John Endicott, were incorporated into John Clarke's *Ill Newes
from New England,* as discussed above (Chapter 2). His three
letters to John Winthrop, Jr. (noted in Chapter 3 above) were never
published, either in his lifetime or subsequently.

His major literary effort, however, is his Testimony, written
chiefly — perhaps entirely — in 1675, seven years before his death.
This manuscript, originally perhaps about sixty pages in length,
has never been published, though Isaac Backus used portions of it
in his uniquely valuable work, *A History of New England with
Particular Reference to the Baptists,* the first volume of which
appeared in 1777. Backus, who describes the Testimony as "the
best account of Mr. Obadiah Holmes that I have seen," borrowed it
from "a gentleman of his posterity,"[1] made his excerpts, and apparently returned it to the unnamed descendant of Obadiah
Holmes. About a century later, Benjamin B. Howland, the town
clerk of Newport, Rhode Island from 1825 to 1875, copied the
Testimony from the autograph copy "lent me by Mr. Henry Bull
whose wife is a descendent of Mr. Holmes, in whose possession are
the original manuscripts."[2] Howland, a deacon in Newport's First
Baptist Church (from 1837 until his death in 1877) and a dedicated
transcriber of early historical records, presented his copy to the
Newport Historical Society in 1868;[3] a little over a half-century later
the original manuscript, now barely legible, also came into the
possession of the Society.[4]

Last Will & Testimony

The Holmes manuscript numbers fifty-two pages in its present form, but several sheets at the end of the small leatherbound notebook are missing. To judge from the page fragments still attached to the binding, some six pages (with writing on both sides) have been torn or cut out. This mutilation occurred before Howland made his copy, for the latter also ends abruptly in the third section of Holmes' "Letter to the World." The Testimony remains, therefore, incomplete — existing only in a single copy from the seventeenth century and that a severely imperfect one. Yet it is by far not only the largest block of writing composed by Holmes, but also the most valuable witness to the theology, the preaching style, the family life, and the personal piety and devotion that we have for any seventeenth-century Baptist in America. More than three hundred years after its composition, it deserves to be read in as full a context as the surviving literary remains allow.

"Literary" perhaps conveys a falsely grandiose notion. Holmes was no literary artist, no creative genius with the pen. He was, in fact, not an educated man and perhaps only late in life a literate one. In a recent study entitled *Literacy in Colonial New England* (New York, 1974), Kenneth A. Lockridge concludes that only about one-half of New England's adult population was literate in 1650, though that proportion rapidly increased to virtually 100 percent by the end of the colonial period. In Holmes' case, moreover, it is evident that he gave his "mark" rather than his signature as late as 1645.[5] In later years, however, Holmes signed deeds, inventories, and his own will. More conclusively, John Clarke spoke of the Holmes letters that appeared in *Ill Newes* as having been "written with his own hand." And while the will appears to have been written by another hand, as was frequently the case with legal documents, the letters to John Winthrop, Jr., as well as the original manuscript of the Testimony, do not suggest the writing of some other, more "cultivated" scribe. One may fairly conclude, therefore, that at least in his later years Obadiah Holmes could both read and write. Just as fairly, however, one can argue that he did neither extensively; the books left in his estate were appraised at a total value of eight shillings — about the cost of a chair or a chest.[6]

One near-contemporary, Deputy Governor (of Rhode Island) Joseph Jenckes, explained the difference in Boston's treatment of Holmes and John Clarke in these words: "Mr. Holmes was whipped thirty stripes . . . but Mr. Clarke, being a Scholar bred, a friend of his paid his fine for him."[7] In Massachusetts gentlemen were not whipped unless "profligate and vicious"; Holmes had neither the social standing nor the literary attainment to merit any special consideration. He stands in contrast, therefore, to his better-known contemporaries Roger Williams and John Clarke, both of whom were products of a university. Williams' association with Pembroke College, Cambridge (A.B., 1627) is well known, as are his seven volumes of writings.[8] John Clarke, partly because his name (in a variety of spellings, of course) is so common, is more difficult to associate with a particular institution with any degree of certainty. One intriguing possible identity is that of a John Clarke who received his Bachelor of Arts degree from Brasenose College, Oxford on November 11, 1628, and his Master of Arts degree on July 2, 1632. If this is the Clarke long associated with Holmes in Newport, then he probably knew one or both of Obadiah's brothers identified as scholars at Brasenose (John Holmes entered on November 18, 1625, Samuel on February 15, 1633).[9] Clarke, in addition to being a physician, demonstrated his command of the ancient languages by composing a complete Bible concordance and lexicon; though the former was advertised for sale in London, it apparently was never published.[10]

One reads Obadiah Holmes, then, for neither showy erudition nor elegant style, but for simplicity and conviction. "Plainness" is one of his favorite words. So that this plainness could more readily emerge, the text has been rendered as readable as possible in accordance with the principles indicated in the Preface. In addition to those principles concerning spelling, punctuation, capitalization and the like, a few other points should be noted here. Word order has occasionally been altered to correspond with modern usage. A few seventeenth-century idioms no longer carrying their earlier meaning have quietly been replaced. Holmes was repeatedly guilty of what a grammar teacher calls "run-on" sentences. These interminable sentences have been broken up, with the result that it has frequently been necessary to add a subject for the new sentence. If that is the only addition, it has been inserted without brackets. But if other words were deemed necessary, these appear within brackets (elements within parentheses are Holmes' own). A final editorial principle concerns biblical language. Holmes' writing is so full of biblical imagery, rhythm, allusion, and phraseology that it would be both tedious and difficult to identify every such reference. Specific identifications have been given, therefore, only when Obadiah Holmes is consciously reciting an extended quotation or close paraphrase of biblical material.

A. Testimony on his Life

THE VALUE OF OBADIAH HOLMES' TESTIMONY IS SEEN INITIALLY AND PERHAPS most powerfully in this autobiographical section. For no other seventeenth-century Baptist in America has left us so detailed an account of his conversion experience. Spiritual autobiography was much "in the air" in this century, but the American examples are chiefly Puritan.[1] On the British side, some Baptist analogues do exist: *The Life and Death of Mr. Vavasor Powell* (1671), a Welsh Baptist preacher; and, far better known, John Bunyan's *Grace Abounding to the Chief of Sinners* (1666). And Bunyan, like Holmes, told of his spiritual struggles with an eye on "plainness." Bunyan writes:

> I could . . . have stepped into a style much higher than this in which I have here discoursed, and could have adorned all things more than here I have seemed to do, but I dare not. God did not play in convincing of me; the Devil did not play in tempting of me; neither did I play when I sunk as into a bottomless pit. . . . Wherefore I may not play in my relating of them, but be plain and simple, and lay down the thing as it was . . . .[2]

Bunyan (1628-1688), born some twenty years after Obadiah Holmes' birth, went through similar spiritual struggles and at roughly the same period of his life. From about eighteen years of age until twenty-three, Bunyan suffered the torments of spiritual doubt and the sense of total unworthiness and condemnation: "I did now feel myself to sink into a gulf" like "some child that was fallen into a mill-pit, who though it could make some shift to scramble and sprawl in the water, yet because it could find neither hold for hand nor foot therefore at last it must die in that condition."[3] But, again like Holmes (as well as Paul and Luther, from whom Bunyan explicitly draws), the resolution came in personal experience, experience of such blinding intensity and enduring reality that doubt was forever driven away: ". . . now I saw clearly

70

there was an exceeding difference betwixt the notions of flesh and blood, and the revelations of God in Heaven; also a great difference between that faith that is feigned and according to man's wisdom, and that which comes by a man being born thereto unto God."[4] Preaching that had formerly wounded him and scripture that had been only a burden now became sweetness and joy: "Now went I also home rejoicing, for the grace and love of God."[5]

Spiritual narratives tend to be vague concerning time and place: the soul's struggle is a cosmic one, timeless and under the stars. Yet, Holmes' reference to his mother's illness and death makes it possible to date his conversion at about 1630, when he (like Bunyan) was about twenty-three years of age. This experience, while making him a Christian, did not at that time make him a Baptist; in fact, no Calvinist Baptist church yet existed in England. His search for a proper or satisfying ecclesiastical home led him to New England, "where I tried all things in several churches" — probably Boston briefly and then Salem. But, as noted above in Chapter 1, not until the "new baptism" reached him in Rehoboth in 1644 did Obadiah Holmes find a form that seemed fully faithful to a total experience of death to sin and new life in God.

In his letter to the London Baptists, Holmes spoke of his "experimental knowledge." Here in his Testimony the point is made even more emphatically that he preaches because of and out of his own experience: "That which first moved me to entreat and beseech them to be reconciled to God was the consideration of God's mercy showed to my poor soul. . . ." There was weakness in not being a man of great learning, but there was also strength, centering, and assurance: I have learned, Holmes writes here, "by the scriptures and experience." What more was needed? And the power of Holmes' testimony is that the "experiment" works, the gospel works: "I have found it made good of me." God also faithfully works: "I have ever found Him as good as His word, and promises never failed me in any difficult time."

With so much emphasis on experience, the danger or the temptation is to dispense with all that is external: churches, ministers, ordinances, and even scriptures. Holmes steers a careful middle course between those who would place too much emphasis on forms (the Seventh Day Baptists) and those who would place too little (the Quakers). Holmes will observe the ordinances, but he will not trust in them: "I use them, but yet my soul's consolation and rest is not in them. . . ." For Baptists, the special temptation was to make a fetish out of baptism. Holmes recognizes the temptation —

71

and resists it. Baptism is a significant ordinance, "which I own and have respect unto, but not therein to trust. . . ."

To trust in any of these externals would be to return to the covenant of works, to surrender again to a mindless or politically inspired conformity to a church imposed by others. Works must come as the fruit of faith, and salvation can come never through any striving or working or right living but only by way of the covenant of grace, "even that New Covenant of life [given] alone by Himself who paid so dear a price. . . ."6

On My Life

THE TWENTIETH DAY OF THE TENTH MONTH [DECEMBER] in the year 1675, Obadiah Holmes now comes to the Testimony of the day. Being sixty-nine years old or thereabouts and wishing to give some account of my estate and condition — what it is, what it was, and what my hopes are that it shall be hereafter, [I write now] unto my friends and relations whether in Old England or New. I have had so many requests and desires from brethren and friends to that end and purposes, and I know not but it may be some occasion to provoke others to try their evidences themselves* and not to take all on trust as I fear many are apt to do. Even the apostle says: Try, prove, examine your own selves; know you not that Christ dwells in you except you be reprobate. † And this has been my great work this fifty years, and yet remains my greatest work.

First, I must remember my honored parents who were faithful in their generation and of good report among men and brought up their children tenderly and honorably. Three sons they brought up at the University of Oxford,‡ but the most of their care was to inform them and instruct them in the fear of the

---

* That is, to test "experimentally" the work of the Spirit in their own lives.
† See 2 Corinthians 13:5.
‡ See above, p. 7.

Lord and, to that end, to give them much good counsel, carrying them often before the Lord by earnest prayer. But I, the most rebellious of all, did hearken neither to counsel nor to any instruction. For, from a child, I minded nothing but folly and vanity. And, as years did grow on, wisdom should have taken place; but the wisdom I had was wise to do evil, but to do well I had no knowledge.

As days and strength increased, even so did my transgressions. I became hardened to sin, not only to be drawn into it by others, but was so forward as to draw others into evil as my fellows. Being come to the height of wickedness, I did think it best that I could do the most wickedness. I began to think it was but a foolish thing to talk of a God that should bring man to judgment; therefore, the best thing for me was to take pleasure in whatever the flesh could content itself, in whatever my heart could desire. Yea, and I had all things concerning and agreeing to that end, accomplishing such wicked desires — and that in strength of body and vanity with all things suitable. Still, my corrupt, vain heart was not yet satisfied. It so ranged abroad that, had I not been prevented, I had thought to have compounded and contracted with the devil for more powerful ways and means to assure such evil ends as I propounded [proposed] to myself.

Continuing in such a course for four or five years, I began to bethink me what counsel my dear parents and my dear mother had given me: many a call, many a time, with tears and prayers. My rebellion to my honored parents then looked me in the open face. And dear Mother, being sick, it struck me that my disobedient acts caused her death, which forced me to confess the same to her — my evil ways. After this time, I began to go hear the word preached, but every word that was spoken was against me and left me without hopes of any mercy. Sometimes, passing over a field called Twenty Acres, I stood still and said: "Oh! that I might lie in hell so many years as here are grass! — it would have an end!" And, at other times looking on the stars of

heaven in the night, I said: "Oh! that I might lie in hell but so
many years as there are stars! — it would have an end!" That
word was ever before me: the wicked shall be turned to hell,
there to be tormented with the devil and his angels forever,
where the worm dieth not, nor the fire ever goeth out. *

Yet at this time Satan told me: It is best for thee to put such
things out of mind and take pleasure while thou are here and
return to thy merry companions. I did for a time, but the worm
in the conscience did still gnaw. I went to hear the most noted
men I could, but found it [the word] still against me. Yet I often
heard them say that I must repent and be humble and pray and
then thee should find mercy. Thee must confess thy sins and
forsake them, and *then* thee shall find mercy. This brought me to
a resolution in the most public way and company I could find so
to do. And [I would have] done it, through ignorance, had not
a friend advised me to the contrary — and that upon good
ground. He also put me upon prayer and duties. I then fell to
prayer and duties, but found no rest or quiet in my soul. Then
Satan let fly at me as an adversary and told me it was too late to
return, for there was no hope for me. I answered him and did
instance several of my wicked companions that God had shown
mercy to but little before. He answered: Remember, thou
scorned and mocked and derided them, yea and cursed them,
saying the devil was in them and they were all mad. Withal, He
told me that I had read and heard that there was a sin which
never should be forgiven in this life nor that which is to come —
which sin I had committed!

With this, even this assault he fooled me a long time, even so
that my life was a burden to me. Oh! the knives, ropes, trees,
coalpits can witness the many escapades of one in a most undone
and desperate condition, as one appointed to eternal destruction here and hereafter. The perplexity of mind brought me to
great weakness in body; yet, for ease and comfort, I turned over
every stone, hearkened to all my acquaintances and friends as to

* See Revelation 20:10 and Isaiah 66:24.

74

leaving of my old ways and all my old companions — which thing I had done before with hatred toward their and my own ways. But all this while I never considered sin according to the true nature of it as huge and loathsome to the Lord, but only as bringing judgment upon me as one man. Yet was I fearful to sin and began to read the scriptures and be frequent in prayer and other duties, and took delight among professors [witnesses to the faith] that were of the strictest sort. [I saw] easily the gross evil of the formal ministers and that conformity* was only a superstition, a name.

For all that, I had no rest in the soul, though I was in the manner strict as any. As I was enlarged in sorrow for sin and deep in humiliation, enlarged in prayer or filled with tears, my comfort came in and increased; but, as I failed in them, so my sorrow was renewed. And when I looked over my best performances and found them full of sin — Oh! then the fear and doubts and questions concerning my own estate. I judged that it was all done in hypocrisy, which sin my soul did abhor. Even in this sad and doubtful† state, I continued very long, yea, many years, and although I could speak comfort to others, yet was I often disquieted in my soul — and so was my comfort according to my enlargements.

Not long after this, there was in me a great love to the Lord, but alas, I was deceived by my own heart. And the ministers who told me that there must be such and such a love to Him as to keep to Him in duty and to part with all for Him still left me short of understanding Him as I should. My selfish heart was willing to love Him and to part with all for Him; yea, with my dear honored father, brethren and friends, house and land, and my own native country for time. [I also determined] to avoid the popish relics of the bishops and that filthy, hellish rabble, and to separate from them and all those that mentioned them and were

* Conformity to the Church of England and specifically to the ritual requirements of the Book of Common Prayer.
† Literally, "filled with doubt."

fully known in my own country. [I determined to] adventure the dangers of the seas to come to New England where I tried all things in several churches. For a time, I thought I had made a good choice or change, but in truth it little differed from former times. My spirit was like a wave tossed up and down — not yet come to dig so deep as I should, or to consider the only ground of a well grounded hope.

God at last brought me to consider [that well grounded hope], which was His own love to poor lost man. [This existed] in His own secret counsel and purpose before man ever was, and was revealed to man in his times. [I understood] that there is no preparation necessary to obtain Christ, nor anything to deserve that love so as to merit the same. Nothing could stay or satisfy [the sinner] when he laid sin and transgression upon the Lord and upon Him alone. God looked at me as a rebel, an enemy, yea, dead in sin and trespasses, yea in my blood. He then said: Live through the blood of Christ, be cleansed and in Him be loved. For His own [love reveals itself] to poor man and the election may obtain it, for He knows who are His. His good will is manifested before men have done either good or evil, so that neither good foreseen nor evil original nor actual shall hinder — so that free grace may have its free course. [This grace is] manifested when one gives faith: to believe the promise of the Father in giving a full discharge to the soul, by taking full satisfaction from His only Son who became sin for us and knew no sin that we might be made the righteousness of God through Him. And so remission and a free pardon is granted forth, that whosoever believes in Him shall not perish but have everlasting life; and all those that so come to Him He will no ways cast away.

When God had given me to see in any measure this love of His, then and not until then could I give over working for life and to live in working. At last He caused me to say *from* life I must work; then, all my former turnings and returnings must come to naught. Yea, all my righteousness is as filthy rags, and to account all as dung so I might obtain Christ, or rather that I might be accepted by Him and so removed from the covenant of works to the covenant of grace — even that New Covenant of life [given] alone by Himself who paid so dear a price as to lay down His own blood to wash, cleanse and purify the soul and to redeem by God both soul and body to serve the Lord. That is now the life I live in by the faith of the Son of God. This faith causes works of faith or, rather, fruit that flows from that root so that now love hath constrained me to yield up myself to live, as to a king, to rule me by His holy laws and commandments; and, as to an only prophet, to teach me and to instruct me both to know and to do his holy will; and, as to my only chief priest, to offer a sacrifice for me which He did even for all, where by [His?] power my imperfect prayers and all other services become accepted of the Father.

This love, shed abroad in my heart, brought in me a restless desire to know His will that I might show forth the praises and glory of Him that had called me by His grace. And though His commandments to the flesh were grievous, they were to my spirit light and ease; yea, and whatever falls in my way heavenward I am content with it. So that in my measure I can say that I have learned to be abased and to abound, to go through good or evil report, to have liberty or restraint, peace or trouble, yea, to live or die is gain. This faith in the Son of God causes me with readiness to yield myself to be obedient to the will of my Lord who has wrought in me both to will and to do His good will and pleasure, and to improve that small talent He gave me for His own use and the profit of those that he called me unto. [I testify] not only for the good of the church at home but for others abroad and for that ever-rested one, my own heart, since He called me forth even to pity poor sinners that they might be informed of the glad tidings from heaven: that God out of His pity and great love sent His Son to save sinners — yea, considered on no other terms but as sinners. That which first moved me to entreat and beseech them to be reconciled to God was the consideration of

God's mercy showed to my poor soul, who was going headlong to the pit of destruction, had not mercy only prevented and free grace only been extended to me. Oh, therefore, I travel in heart day and night in my spirit until Christ be formed in Man; I labor by prayers both day and night that the elect may be called and that God would send laborers into the harvest. For the harvest is great but the laborers few that are found diligent, careful and faithful in the work and service of the Lord.

Many there be in New England that serve themselves and their own backs and bellies, but starve the people. Yet, let my careful duty of love be never so great and rewarded with never so much respect or dishonor (refused or received it is all one to me, for I am but a servant), but the honor alone belongs only to the Lord and their own selves. It is therefore the Lord alone who must teach men to preach. I must tell you that it has been a most hard and difficult lesson to learn: to know my own heart. It has been so deceitful that I could not find it out until the Lord brought me to understand that I must receive eye salve only from Him who alone was the discoverer of secrets. The trouble of the inward parts and what He only wrought that was good was wrought by His Holy Spirit. I have learned that if I want anything that was good, it was from and by Him. That led down my proud flesh, [as I learned] to only glory in the Lord. In truth, when I had the most incomings of God in prayer or speaking as often I met with, even then it was my time to be upon the watch lest the glory had been given to another. I have found that I never could fully quiet my spirit in the most excellent performance, though the matter and form of them were according to the revealed will of God. In the good that I propounded (which as I say proceeds from me as a corrupt and dirty channel), I must disown [the glories] and pray for forgiveness of sin in them. Then, I looked up to Christ to sweeten [my efforts?], that is to say, that the Lord might look down upon me to remember He had taken satisfaction in His own son whom

78

He did offer up: that one sacrifice forever to perfect them that are sanctified in Christ Jesus.

Were it not for that, much and very much discouragement would rest upon me. And I am constrained, though I be in the practice and profession of ordinances according to the revealed will of God, yet to look through them and above them only to the Lord, the Author and Appointer of them to Himself and to find my profession to be in Him and not in them. For I look at every ordinance of His to be but as a means of His own appointment to convey and communicate Himself through those who are but mere men that cannot see the face of God and live. Wherefore, remove me from all the curse of the law and from all righteousness of man to trust only in the Lord. When I began once to look into or trust my own righteousness, alas I found it was dangerous and it greatly took away even that glory that was due to the Lord. For if I did anything worthy of taking notice of, it was but my duty and due debt. So now I am come to see plainly that I am nothing and can do nothing, for in me dwells no good thing. For when I would do good, evil is present with me; and yet I know it is no more I but sin that dwells in my flesh, finding a law in my members rebelling against the law of my mind — which has caused me to cry out: "Oh wretched man that I am, who shall deliver me from the body of this death?"* But in hope and good assurance, I can say: "I thank God through Jesus Christ, our Lord, that I myself in my mind serve the law of God, but in my flesh the law of sin."† I have also learned by the scriptures and experience to see the emptiness and vanity in all things, both men and creatures which I sometimes too much trusted unto. In former days, these have deceived me, so [I know that] nothing in the world below besides the Lord will stand the soul in good stead in a needful time. Though I desire to esteem and account

* See Romans 7:24.
† See Romans 8:1-8.

of men according to what of God I find in them and to own that to His praise, I have seen that it is an evil to make men the strength of counsel or help; and taking men's words in order to [find] a spiritual way of direction is not safe. For the way is to try the spirits, for every spirit is not of God, and he who speaks not according to the Holy Scriptures does so because he has no light in them. Whereupon, I have only them and them alone for my rule and direction, beseeching the Lord to give me understanding of them by His Holy Spirit which is the only revealer of secrets to my soul. [The Holy Spirit] speaks peace to my conscience and that makes me bold, not much mattering what men speak of me, whether good or evil — knowing man who is many times partial in judgment and weak in sight, sometimes calling evil good and good evil, and so passes wrong judgment.

And as I find emptiness in man, so [I find] emptiness and want in all creatures. As for honor among men, that vanity is high. Dignities, vain things, riches are vain — taking their wings, and they are gone. Strength and beauty are vain, long-life burdensome; creature comforts are empty stubble; nothing here below but doth admit of trouble and vexation of spirit. Therefore, my desire is neither to covet one thing or another to serve as my rest or comfort or thereon to trust. But [I regard all] as a staff in my weak hand for present help, and that no farther than the Lord shall make any creature for my present use: and so to possess as if not, and to judge as not judging anything, for my life and living is the fountain of life — the Lord Jesus Christ. For the Lord has given me His Son: how shall He not with Him give me all things that He sees needful for me, so that I need not to say what shall I eat or wherewith shall I be clothed, or be in doubtful despair, for He is my all and has said that He is all sufficient. And even when my soul is troubled desiring such and such a temptation to be removed, even then He as it were answers me that His grace is sufficient for me. And I have found it made good to me: altering, proving, removing or delivering out according to His good pleasure. So that I have ever found Him as good as His word, and promises never failed me in any difficult time. When I was beset either with Satan or with his instruments in my suffering condition, [God's] rod and staff did comfort me and did refresh my soul. At times when men wrote or spoke hard things against me, He then spoke peace and upheld a weak body to bear what men could lay upon it — and that with ease and comfort. I never was in any strait but the Lord was my present help in any difficult time; and though I have passed through many trials the word of the Lord was my stay, through the help of the Holy Spirit from which I have received sweet consolation. And though my heart and affections and judgment and practice is to ordinances, as they are God's own appointment and commandment in obedience to the Lord — I use them, but yet my soul's consolation and rest is not in them, but in the Lord Himself and His own conveyance of Himself through them. For they are no more profitable to my soul than as conveyances of Himself to me, and that in them I have possession of Him who is my life.

If I may give you an account of a secret (though to many it is not a secret), it is this. When I have been in the most enjoyment of ordinances and most affected and enlarged in any performance, I have been even then in the most danger of a great evil if not the worst sin: namely, to take away that glory from God and to take the honor to myself, or at best to rest quiet as if that should have been my only support. Therefore, the Lord knows what strugglings and strivings and examining of my own heart have I had after my nearest approaches; and, when I was gotten in any esteem among men and upon these tongues of prayer, then was a time for me to be upon watch and truly then was I most thrown down in myself, and have thought really that I was the least of sinners, but truly the chief of sinners.

Nothing in the world lay more upon my spirit than sin. Often, yea very often, I desired the Lord to give forth to my spiritual understanding the power and virtue and benefit of the blood of Christ to cleanse and wash me from all my sin. I [wished] more and more to find the good effect of that significant ordinance of baptism which I own and have respect unto, but not therein to trust, but yet good in its place as other appointments of the Lord. None of them [is] to be neglected or slighted by any that find the Lord and love Him in sincerity and truth. It is my desire that while I am in the land of the living I may use them in obedience and love to my Lord and in a careful, earnest waiting for His own Spirit in and through them. As for the Spirit of the Lord, it is the only Comforter, and gives the only true and certain [words missing] to my soul in order with my peace to God and union and fellowship with Him and in that eternal and everlasting glory.

Oh, that He has laid down His life and did undergo that death, even the cursed death upon the cross, to free me from sin and so to bring me to glory! The first cause of this was the purpose of God in His decree and counsel before the foundation of the world. Even then He found a way whereby mercy and justice might meet, truth and peace might kiss each other. And while I am in this conflict and spiritual battle I might have hope for my salvation as first appointed in that decree of God's; second, it was by means of the Lord Jesus Christ; and, in the third place, [it was] witnessed to me by the Spirit and through faith in Jesus and [was] declared to man by word and deed in life and conversation to the comfort of others who were partakers of the same grace.

Now, to the Lord alone be all honor and glory forever and ever, Amen.

B. Testimony of his Faith

BAPTISTS HAD NO NECESSARY OBJECTION TO CREEDS OR CONFESSIONS OF faith; they merely objected to having them imposed by others. An individual, a church, a group of churches felt entirely free, however, to affirm its belief and to proclaim it boldly. Obadiah Holmes was moved to offer his credo, not only because he had "come to the evening of the day," but because he had been specifically asked by a few friends or relatives to do so. Among those requesting this was his brother, Robert Holmes, who had inherited the family farm in Reddish and who had maintained an active role in Gorton Chapel nearby.[1] Indeed, the concluding postscript — or instructions to the postman — provides critical clues to Holmes' ancestry and place of origin. Although Holmes had left England almost forty years before, he had not been forgotten; and religious issues, as well as the progress of many pilgrims, were still lively concerns in and around Manchester.

Understandably, Holmes' confession of faith makes many of the same points enunciated in the confessions of other early Baptists, both in America and abroad. The influential London Confession of 1644, signed by William Kiffin and John Spilsbury among others, spells out some fifty-three articles of faith in about four times the length which Holmes uses for his thirty-five points.[2] And in 1665 the Baptist church in Boston offered the Massachusetts authorities a brief outline of "their faith and order proved from the word of God."[3] But each of these confessions also served a major defensive purpose: in London, the seven Particular Baptist Churches attempted to put a good deal of distance between themselves and the more radical continental Anabaptists with whom they were being deliberately and continuously confused; in Boston, the one beleaguered Baptist church tried to convince the Puritan citizenry that they too were a truly biblical, truly responsible church of Jesus Christ. In 1675, Holmes no longer worried about the magistrates nor did he feel obliged to protest that Baptists can be loyal citizens also. His Testimony, in fact, ignores the civil domain and otherwise shows little or no dependence on the confessions of his coreligionists.[4] It is his faith and his voice.

That faith stands unmistakably in the Calvinist tradition, as did that of the London churches, the Boston church, and the whole surrounding and dominating Puritan culture. As in Puritan theology, Holmes' Calvinism was expressed through the vehicle of a covenant of grace that displaced and made forever obsolete the old covenant of works which God had made with Adam. The New Testament revealed the New Covenant, a new and precious relationship with God now made possible by, and only by, the life, death, and resurrection of Jesus Christ. That remarkable work of Christ — and this, of course, is *the* good news, *the* gospel par excellence — was prefigured in the Old Testament "in dark shadows and types,"[5] but was fully revealed only in the new age, the new era, the new dispensation through the atoning sacrifice of Christ: ". . . by the shedding of His precious blood is my redemption, and not mine only but all that are or shall be saved."

Those destined to be saved are, to be sure, those whom God chooses to save, his elect, "for He knows who are His. . . ." And because man does not save himself, he cannot cause himself to be lost. All that are in the covenant of grace "shall never fall away or perish." The saints persevere because God does not weaken or change. Those who come to him he will in no way and at no time cast out. Calvinist Baptists in London (William Kiffin among them) endorsed the small pamphlet published by Boston's pastor, John Russell, in 1680 (*A Brief Narrative* . . .), saying that the Boston Baptists "have declared their perfect agreement with us both in matters of faith and worship, as set down in our late confession."[6] And a later Newport pastor provided an abstract of "a small book written by John Clarke . . . containing his judgment and the judgment of the Church respecting that soul supporting doctrine of personal election. . . ."[7] The Calvinist character of these New England Baptists in the seventeenth century is thus apparent, and the Testimony of Obadiah Holmes places him centrally in that tradition.

Naturally, an all-sovereign God can save men in any way that he chooses, "yet He has appointed an ordinary way to effect that great work of faith which is by means of sending a ministry into the world. . . ." Contrary to Roger Williams, Holmes believed that the work of the church and its ministry was still valid, still ordained of God, even in this wicked and nonapostolic age. But this ministry, declared Holmes, is to preach Scripture and not "a mission of their own brain." Moreover, they are not to take up the holy task "without a special call from God" and, if called, they are to take it without any motive for gain. Since the minister "has received freely of the Lord, so he is freely to give." Christ's great commission to the minister is that he go forth, make disciples, and baptize, "but not to baptize them before they believe." Only in the proper sequence, then, is one able to administer a true gospel baptism, which "is a visible believer with his own consent being baptized in common water [i.e., not holy water] by dipping," or symbolically being "drowned to hold forth [the] death, burial, resurrection" of Christ.

The minister, however, is but a single and imperfect instrument. Even more significant in God's grand scheme is the ministry of the congregation, "a people called out of the world by the word and spirit of the Lord." This "holy brotherhood" is to wait upon the Holy Spirit, keep its fellowship pure, break bread together, pray, serve, teach, and "prophesy one by one." All members are to use whatever talents God has given them, looking and waiting for that day firmly promised when they shall "enter into the joy of [their] Lord" — a joy far beyond anything known to the senses or even to the imagination of earth-bound mortals.

Of My Faith

NOW CONSIDERING THAT I HAVE COME TO THE EVENING of the day [when] I may expect my change every moment, the great desolations in this day cause me to consider what is my hope and expectation for another life immortal, forever, yea everlasting.

The hope that I have is grounded only upon the decreed purpose and counsel of God before man was. God alone appointed and determined what should come to pass in His appointed time. Of Himself and by His might of wisdom and abundant love, He brought forth life and immortality into light by Jesus Christ and laid the iniquity of man upon Him — yea, of all men that are to be saved. By His death and His death alone comes my hope of eternal life through Him, so that I rest in hope while I suffer under many foul temptations and alterations in this present evil world. After a little while of suffering I shall lay down this my earthly tabernacle of clay, and yet am comforted in the hopes of the glory and happy resurrection to meet my Lord. Though I now see Him not, yet love Him and His appearance, then shall I behold His power and glory in the ruling over of his enemies and reign with His people a thousand years. Then will the end be, and then will the Lord deliver His kingdom into His Father's hand. Then that glory shall be manifested, possessed and enjoyed which eye has not seen, ear has not heard, neither has it entered into the heart of man — the joy God has prepared for them that love and fear the Lord. The consideration of those things makes me to joy in tribulations, patient in hope, and in hopeful expectation of that endless glory with the Father, Son and Holy Angels and Glorified Saints which is the fulfilling of the good pleasure of the Lord, unto whom be honor, glory and praise forever and ever.

The Lord moved my heart to write these lines that they might speak forth my mind if I should lie down in silence, or if I should be taken away suddenly by the enemy, or die with sickness and my senses or memory should fail me. [I write now] that my dear and near relations and my brethren natural or spiritual and the world may know that I was what I am, and what I am and expect to be and enjoy. It may be that some may make but a scorn of what is written, and others slight the same, but it may be that some may ponder and weigh the same. If any receive either information or comfort, give the glory unto the Lord forever and ever, Amen.

Be ready to give a reason of the hope that is in you with reverence and fear, says the Apostle. * Having had two or three requests or invitations from you my friends and brethren, and

* See I Peter 3:15.

86

especially my brother Robert,* to give you some information of my present state or standing with reference to the Lord and my own soul, I shall as briefly as I can give account thereof unto you whom I trust will either rejoice with me or yet consider your own standing and farther acquaint me with your condition.

But before I come to speak to the point at hand, I cannot forget the rock out of which I was hewn and the cistern out of which I was digged. I was by nature a child of wrath as [much] as others, and by actual transgression added sin to sin as my conscience and others did know, but God had mercy for me in store when I neither deserved it nor desired it. For He knows who are His and the elect shall obtain it forever. Blessed be His holy name, to whom be glory forever, Amen.

Now in this faith or belief I stand, not doubting but it is the faith of God's elect, for He knows who are His and the elect shall obtain it.

First, I believe there is one essence or being, even one God who made heaven and earth, the waters and all things therein contained, who by His own divine power governs all things by the same word of His power, and has appointed life and death to men and bounded their habitations, whose Providence extends to the least creature and actions.

2. I believe this God is Father to one Lord Jesus Christ, and in a special understanding may be distinguished as Father, Son and Holy Spirit and yet but one in essence.

3. I believe that as God made the world, so by His word made He man in his own image, without sin, and gave him a most excellent place and being, giving him commandments what he should do and what he should forbear; but, through the malice of Satan working with his wife, he was deceived. For she did eat and gave her husband and he did eat, which was the first cause of the curse to him and reached to all his posterity by which came death natural and death eternal.

* See introduction to this section above.

4. I believe in this interim of time that the Lord manifested His great love in that word, "The seed of the woman shall break the head of the serpent,"* but enmity was between the two seeds.

5. I believe that at that and later times the Lord was worshipped by sacrifices, though darkly held forth to us.

6. I believe that, after that time, God in His own time chose a people to Himself and gave them His laws and statutes in a special manner, though He had always His chosen ones in every generation.

7. I believe that with this people He made a choice covenant to be their God and they to be His people, which covenant they broke, though He was a Father to them and was grieved for them. Yet not only did He give them His laws, but sent His prophets early and late, but they would not hear. And, in the fullness of time, He sent His only Son, but as they had abused His prophets, so they killed His only Son.

8. I believe that God in His Son made a new covenant, a sure everlasting covenant, not like He had made with Israel (of which Moses, that faithful servant, was mediator); but a covenant of grace and peace through His only Son, that whosoever believed in Him should not perish but have everlasting life.

9. I believe that all those that are in this covenant of grace shall never fall away nor perish, but shall have life in the Prince of life: the Lord Jesus Christ.

10. I believe that no man can come to the Son but they that are drawn by the Father to Him, and they that come He will in no wise cast away.

11. I believe He came to call sinners to repentance, for the whole need not, but they that are sick.

12. I believe that by the shedding of His precious blood is my redemption, and not mine only but all that are or shall be saved.

13. I believe that as He is God so was He man, for He did not take the nature of angels but the nature of Abraham.

---

* See Genesis 3:15.

14. I believe that God has laid the iniquity of all His elect and called ones upon Him.

15. I believe that the Father is fully satisfied and the debt is truly paid to the utmost farthing, and the poor sinner is quit and set free from all sin, past, present and to come.

16. I believe the Holy Scriptures which testify of Christ in dark shadows and types, and all that was written of Christ in the prophets and psalms, and that He was born of a virgin at Bethlehem, and came to His own and they received Him not.

17. I believe He was put to death and hanged upon a tree called the cross, and was buried, and the third day rose again according to the Scriptures, and appeared to many as is witnessed in the Scriptures.

18. I believe He ascended to His Father and sits at his right hand, having made request for His.

19. I believe the Father's commandment and His declaration of Him is to be observed when the Father uttered that voice saying, "This is my beloved Son in whom I am well pleased; hear yet Him."*

20. I believe there is no salvation but by Him alone, no other Name under heaven by which man can be saved.

21. I believe He is sent unto the world and to be published to all men, but some — yea, many — resist the counsel of God against themselves.

22. I believe none has power to choose salvation or to believe in Christ, for life is the gift only of God.

23. I believe that although God can bring men to Christ and cause them to believe in Him for life, yet He has appointed an ordinary way to effect that great work of faith which is by means of sending a ministry into the world to publish repentance to the sinner and salvation, and that by Jesus Christ. They that are faithful shall save their own souls and some that hear them.

24. I believe that they that are sent of God are not to declare a mission of their own brain, but as it is in the Scripture

* See Matthew 3:17; Mark 1:11; and Luke 3:22.

of truth; for holy men wrote them as they were inspired by the Holy Spirit.

25. I believe that the precious gift of the Spirit's teaching was procured by Christ's ascension and given to men, begetting of souls to the truth and for the establishment and consolations of those that are turned to the Lord. For none shall pluck them out of His Father's hands: He is greater than all.

26. I believe that no man is to rush into the ministry without a special call from God, even as the Gospel ministers had of old. [This] was the call of the Holy Spirit with some talent or talents to declare the counsel of God to poor sinners, declaring the grace of God through Jesus Christ even to those that are yet in the power of Satan, yea, to bring glad tidings by and from the Lord Jesus Christ.

27. I believe that this ministry is to go forth and he that has received grace with a talent or talents, as he has received freely of the Lord so he is freely to give, looking for nothing to gain but the promise of the Lord.

28. I believe that none is to go forth but by commission, and carefully to observe the same according as Christ gave it forth, without adding or diminishing: first, to preach Christ (that is, to make disciples), and then, to baptize them — but not to baptize them before they believe; and, then, to teach them what Christ commanded them, for as the Father had his order in the former dispensation and administration, so has the Son (in former times, the Lord spoke in divers way and manners, but now has He spoken by His Son).

29. I believe that as God prepared a begetting ministry, even so does He also prepare a feeding ministry in the church, who are a people called out of the world by the word and Spirit of the Lord, assembling themselves together in a holy brotherhood, continuing in the apostles' doctrine and fellowship, breaking bread and prayer.

30. I believe that such a church or company ought to wait for the Holy Spirit of promise, on whom it may fall, and to

choose out among themselves either pastor, teacher or elders to rule, or deacons to serve the table, that others may give themselves to the word and prayer and to keep them close to the Lord and their fellowship clear and distinct — not to have fellowship with the unfruitful workers of darkness but rather to reprove them.

31. I believe that the Church of Christ or this company so gathered are bound to wait on the Lord for the Spirit to help them, and have liberty and are under duty that they may prophesy one by one.

32. I believe that the true baptism of the Gospel is a visible believer with his own consent being baptized in common water by dipping or, as it were, drowned to hold forth death, burial, resurrection, by a messenger of Jesus into the name of the Father, Son and Holy Spirit.

33. I believe the promise of the Father concerning the return of Israel and Judah, and the coming of the Lord to raise up the dead in Christ, and to change them that are alive that they may reign with Him a thousand years, according to the Scriptures.

34. I believe the resurrection of the wicked to receive their just judgment: go, ye cursed, to the devil and his angels forever.

35. I believe as eternal judgment to the wicked, so I believe the glorious declaration of the Lord saying, "Come, ye blessed of my Father; enter into the joy of your Lord, which joy eye has not seen, ear has not heard; neither can it enter into the heart to conceive the glory that God has prepared for them that love and wait for His appearance. Wherefore, come Lord Jesus, come quickly." *

For this faith and profession I stand and have sealed the same with my blood at Boston in New England, † and hope through the strength of my Lord to be able to witness the same to death.

* See I Corinthians 2:9; II Timothy 4:8; Revelation 22:20.

† This is Holmes' only reference, throughout the entire Testimony, to his public whipping in Boston (see above, pp. 28f.).

[This remains my faith and my hope] although I am a poor unworthy creature, and all my righteousness are as filthy rags and I have nothing to plead or say or fly to but to grace, and have nothing to rest on but only on the free mercy of God, in and through Jesus Christ, my Lord and Savior, to whom be honor, glory and praise, forever and ever, Amen.

Thus have I given you an humble and true account of my standing and of my dear wife standing in one faith and order, that you may consider the same, comparing what is written by the Holy Scriptures which are highly esteemed as our rule towards God and man, committing this and you to the wisdom and counsel of God. Yours in all love to serve continually, having you in our prayers. Fare ye well.

(This is for Mr. John Angher and my brother Robert Holmes, and brother-in-law and sisters, with Mary Honly, and to them that love and fear the Lord. For Robert Holmes at his house in Reddish, near Gorton Chapel, in the parish of Manchester: this deliver with care in Lancashire.)

C. *Testimony to his Wife*

OBADIAH AND CATHERINE HOLMES ENJOYED A LONG AND FRUITFUL MARRIAGE: over fifty years of life together and eight children who grew to maturity. Given the number of women who died in childbirth (or from causes related thereto) and the number of children who never survived infancy, it was a remarkably fortunate marriage.[1] Reading Holmes' "letter to his dear wife" leaves one with the clear impression of a tender and loving relationship. Yet, like most marriages, it was probably not without its strains. Thomas Cobbet (see above, p. 15) stated that Holmes' own wife was among those reproving him for his behavior at Rehoboth, and Catherine's name is notably absent from the list of those who withdrew from the established church there to form the nucleus of a private Baptist fellowship. (Also, the records of the Salem church speak of Obadiah as "excommunicated" but describe Catherine merely as "removed.")[2] Even more strangely, the name of Catherine Holmes does not appear in the membership lists of the Newport church. Yet, in the testimony of his faith Holmes concludes: "Thus have I given you an humble and true account of my standing and of my dear wife's standing in one faith and order. . . ." One can only surmise — and that most tentatively — that while no basic theological difference existed between the two, Catherine was more reluctant to support a competing or novel ecclesiastical structure.

This situation apparently also obtained between Roger Williams and his wife, Mary. Mary continued to attend the Puritan church in Salem long after her husband had withdrawn, until, in the words of John Cotton, "at length he drew her to partake with him in the error of his way."[3] Also like Holmes, Williams wrote a letter of comfort and consolation to his wife, though Williams' composition, *Experiments of Spiritual Life & Health,* was in fact a small treatise that found its way into print in London in 1652. Williams wrote not in anticipation of his impending death but out of concern for his long absences from his wife and for her occasional spiritual desolation. Nonetheless, Williams' long letter, like Holmes' shorter one, is a preparation for or meditation upon death. For while one may find comfort in this world, one must be ever ready to leave it.

> God's children — as travelers on the land, as passengers on a ship — must use this world and all the comforts of it with dead and weaned and mortified affections, as if they used them not. If riches, if children, if cattle, if friends, if whatsoever increase, let us watch that the heart fly not loose upon them. As we use salt with raw and fresh meats, let us use no worldly comfort without a savory remembrance that these worldly goods and comforts are the common portion of the men of this perishing world, who must perish together with them. . . . As the soldier meditates upon the glory of his victories; the sick passenger at sea upon his sweet refreshings on shore; the traveler upon his journey's end and comforts at home; the laborer and hireling on his wages; the husbandman on his harvest; the merchant on his gain; the woman in travail on her fruit, so let us sometimes warm and revive our cold hearts and fainting spirits with the assured hope of those victories, those crowns, those harvests, those refreshings and fruits, which never eye hath seen, nor ear hath heard, nor ever entered into man's heart the things which God hath prepared for them that love him.[4]

"My dear love," Roger Williams concludes, "let us go down together by the steps of holy meditation into the valley of the shadow of death," remembering above all else that "as our sowing is, so shall be our eternal harvest."[5]

In a similar vein, Holmes reminds his "dear love" of all the earthly blessings which God has bestowed upon them, but that "the choice particular favor" which God granted was "in choosing and calling thee to the knowledge of Himself. . . ." No reason can be found, then, for desolation or disquiet — not even after Obadiah, her companion for so many years, is dead and she is alone. Let God then be unto her both husband and heavenly father who "loveth to the end." Moreover, if we both can understand the true nature of death, we then will only rejoice when one of us is "out of all dangers, freed from sin and Satan and all enemies and doubts" and present with the Lord. Holmes also encourages a "holy meditation"; "improve every season for thy soul's advantage," and be not concerned for the things of this world. Remember, God alone "is a sufficient portion."

Yet, Obadiah Holmes is touchingly concerned about the comfort — physical, mental, and spiritual — of his wife. "Now that thou are weak and aged, cease from thy labor and great trial, and take a

94

little rest in thy old age." Holmes makes clear that everything which they have owned together is hers to enjoy and use as long as her life shall last. He insistently explains that she is not to scrimp or deny herself, but at last to use and enjoy: "Make much of thyself." And "sorrow not at my departure, but rejoice. . . ." Obadiah did precede Catherine in death, but apparently not by many months. The early records only say, "She did not long survive him."[6]

To My Wife

A letter to my dear wife, if she remain in the land of the living after my departure, as a true token of my love unto her.

MY MOST DEAR WIFE,

My heart has ever cleaved to thee, ever since we came together, and is knit to thee in death which is the cause of these lines as a remembrance of God's goodness to us in continuing us together almost forty [fifty] years (not diminishing us in our offspring since the first day until now, only our first born*). God has made all our conditions comfortable to us, whether in fullness or emptiness, lifted up or thrown down, in honor or disgrace, sickness or health, by giving us contentment and love one with and to another. But more in a special manner [God has blessed us] in causing His fear to fall upon us and His love to be placed in our hearts and to know His will and to conform up to the obedience of the same — as to be willing to take up the cross and to follow the Lord, not fearing what man can do unto us. For the Lord being on our side, who can be against us? For with His rod and His staff he has comforted us. Yea, He has been our present help in a needful time, and we have cause while we live to praise His holy name while we are together. And when

* See above, p. 9, concerning the infant son buried in England.

death does separate us, may the one still living praise Him while breath remains.

Wherefore, having some thought that I may go away before thee, having signs or token that my day is but short and it may fall out that I cannot or may not speak to thee at the last, I shall give thee some considerations for thy meditations in a time of trouble or affliction — that they may speak when I cannot (if the Lord is pleased to speak in them and by them).

Consider how the Lord carried thee along ever since thou had a being in this world, as by tender parents and since thou came from them, the Lord has provided for thee and preserved thee in many dangers both by sea and land, and has given thee food and raiment with contentment. He has increased our store, sometimes to our admiration [wonder?], also continuing our health in very great measure. He has given us a great posterity who have increased to a great number and has provided for them in a comfortable manner. And the Lord has kept them from such evils as might have befallen them to our grief, but we have had comfort in them. Also, consider the peace we have enjoyed and love we have obtained from our friends and our neighbors and strangers.

Yet, my dear wife, those things are but common favors that many may have their part in. But consider that the choice particular favor that many receive not which God has given to thee in choosing and calling thee to the knowledge of Himself and His dear Son which is life eternal. [So, do] order thy heart to cleave to Him alone, esteeming Him as the chief good, as a pearl of great price, as worthy and causing thy heart to part with all for Him. His love has continued [to help] thee to hearken to His voice, inquiring about His will, so that thou might obey His holy will and commandments, so as to serve Him in thy generation. Oh, consider that great love of the Lord, to cause thy soul to cleave to Him alone and so He to be thy only protection! Having given thee His Son, He has with

Him given thee all things thou dost enjoy, and so to be to thee —
both in life and in death — thy advantage.

The consideration of this causes me to put thee now in mind,
when I am removed, to consider Him as thy husband, as thy
father, as thy Lord and Savior who has said that whom He
loveth, He loveth to the end. And He will not leave them, nor
forsake them, either in the six or seven troubles, * but carry thee
through all, until he bring thee to glory. Wherefore, lift up thy
head and be not discouraged. Say to thy soul, "Why are thou
disquieted within me? Hope in God and trust in His name,"†
and thou shall not be disappointed. Let thy love to me end in
this: that it is better for me to be out of the body and to be with
the Lord at rest with Him and to be freed from that body of sin
and death which I was in while I was in this present evil world.
[That body] caused much sorrow of heart to me in secret; for,
when I would do good, evil was present with me. And consider
the fears you had concerning me every day both for pains and
weakness and dangers, of the many troubles that might befall
me. But now let thy soul say, He is out of all dangers, freed
from sin and Satan and all enemies and doubts; and death is
past and he is at rest in a bed of quietness (as to the body) and
with the Lord in spirit. And at the resurrection, that weak
corrupt mortal body shall be raised immortal and glorious and
shall see and know as he is known. Therefore, say, Why shall I
mourn as one without hope? Rather, rejoice in hope of the
glorious resurrection of the just.

And now, my dear wife, do thou live by the faith of the son
of God, exercise patience, and let patience have its perfect work
in thee. It will be but a little while before thy day will end and
thy time come to sleep with me in rest. He that will come *will
come* and will not tarry. Keep close to the Lord in secret, be

---

* The six troubles described in the Book of Revelation (6:1-8:6 and 8:7-11:19)
followed by a seventh there and in 15:1-16:21.
† See Psalms 42:5.

much with God in prayer, and improve every season for thy soul's advantage, especially in holy meditations. Be cheerful and rejoice in God continually. Care not for the things of this world: say not, What shall I eat or wherewith shall I be clothed, for thy Father knoweth what thou hast need of. And He has given thee much more of these things than ever thou and I could expect or have deserved, and thou hast enough and to spare if His good pleasure be to let thee enjoy the same. If not, He alone is a sufficient portion. Yet, I question not but that He will preserve what thou hast, and bless it to thee. Wherefore, make use of that which He is pleased to let thee enjoy — I say, make use of it for thy present comfort.

Now that thou art weak and aged, cease from thy labor and great trial, and take a little rest and ease in thy old age. Live on what thou hast, for what the Lord has given us, I freely have given thee for thy life, to make thy life comfortable. Wherefore, see that thou dost [enjoy?] it so long as house, land, or cattle remain. Make much of thyself. At thy death, then, what remains may be disposed of according to my will.

And now, my dear wife whom I love as my own soul, I commit thee to the Lord who has been a gracious, merciful God to us all our days, not once doubting but He will be gracious to thee in life — or death. He will carry thee through the valley of tears with His own supporting hand. Sorrow not at my departure, but rejoice in the Lord, and again I say rejoice in the God of our salvation. In nothing be careful [anxious], but make thy request to Him who only is able to supply thy necessities and to help thee in time of need. Unto Whom I commit thee for counsel, wisdom and strength, and to keep thee blameless to the coming of the Lord Jesus Christ, to Whom be all glory, honor and praise forever and ever, Amen. Fare thee well.

D. *Testimony to his Children*

VERY PROBABLY OBADIAH HOLMES' POSTERITY WAS HIS GREATEST LEGACY. His nine children presented him with some forty-one grandchildren. If that rate of productivity continued to the end of the colonial period, Obadiah and Catherine Holmes would have been responsible by that time for a progeny of more than twenty thousand persons! It is, of course, impossible to follow more than a couple of lines. Of the immediate children, four migrated south, either to Gravesend on Long Island or across Lower New York Bay into New Jersey, forming there a settlement named Middletown in honor of the Rhode Island home. Among the twelve original patentees of Monmouth County, New Jersey were Obadiah Holmes, Jr. and John Bowne, the husband of Lydia Holmes. Obadiah, Jr. later settled in Cohansey (West Jersey), which became a major Baptist center; he served as a lay preacher as well as "at the time of his death in 1723 a judge of common pleas for Salem County."[1] Jonathan Holmes also settled in Middletown, where he was elected deputy to the New Jersey assembly in 1668. A decade later he and John Bowne served on the Middletown-Shrewsbury court. Bowne, in fact, later became "a great figure in East Jersey."[2] And it is through Lydia and John Bowne that the senior Obadiah Holmes stands as an ancestor of Abraham Lincoln.[3]

Mary Holmes, the eldest daughter, married John Browne, son of Chad Brown, the Baptist minister in Providence, Rhode Island. From this union emerged the remarkable "Browns of Providence Plantations," that family so central to the economic, cultural, and educational life of the colony-state from that day to this.[4] The second daughter, Martha, married a man named Odlin, a fact known only through the reference to her in her father's will. The same minimal information is available for the youngest daughter, Hopestill, who married a Taylor and died sometime before her father made out his final will in 1681. Samuel Holmes, who also died before his father did (in 1679), was, along with his wife, among those migrating to Gravesend. John Holmes apparently remained in the Rhode Island region, for he witnessed a land sale by John and Mary Browne in 1669;[5] he was twice married and the father of nine children. Jonathan Holmes, also the father of nine children, purchased the family farm (see Section G, below), returned to Newport and joined his father's church. He was not the eldest son, but was probably chosen because he could make the desired financial settlement. Jonathan in turn left the farm to his son, Joseph, who expanded the holdings considerably, leaving an estate valued at nearly £8000 (compared with the estate of his grandfather, valued at about £130).[6] In Rhode Island, New York, and New Jersey, and ultimately in the nation that Obadiah Holmes never knew, his children — and their children's children — came to constitute an imposing monument.

In colonial New England, among Puritans and Baptists alike, a parent was expected to offer counsel and wisdom to his children before his death. Richard Mather, for example, wrote of his "beloved sons" near the end of his life:

> . . . I think it not amiss, for the furtherance of their spiritual good, to lay upon them this serious and solemn charge of a dying Father, that none of them presume, after my decease, to walk in any other way of sin or wickedness, in one kind or in another, or in a careless neglect of God or of the things of God and of their own salvation by Christ. . . .[7]

Roger Clap began his memoirs in this fashion: "I thought good, my dear children, to leave with you some account of God's remarkable providences to me. . . . The Scripture requires us to tell God's wondrous works to our children that they may tell them to their children, that God may have glory throughout all ages."[8] And it was far better for a father to speak the words too early — in Holmes' case, seven years before his death — than to wait until it was too late. John Barnard's father delayed too long, and his son noted in his diary: "He spake but a few words which is a very great aggravation of my sorrow; had it pleased God to have given him the use of his tongue, he might have spoken something that might have had a great and lasting impression upon my heart. . . ."[9]

Obadiah Holmes thus followed a respected and pervasive tradition as he faithfully discharged this serious paternal duty. In writing to his children, some of whom were "in Christ" and some of whom (judging from external appearances) were not, Holmes reminds

100

them of the biblical models for whom they are named. Biblical names were bestowed not just because they were familiar or conveniently "at hand," but because they held forth a standard and a goal by which one's growth in "wisdom and in stature" might be measured. The family enjoyed a closeness which Holmes hoped would not be shattered by his death; he enjoined that their love, one to another, "continue and increase . . . visit one another . . . take counsel one of another . . . advise . . . reprove . . . and take it well."

As was the case in the Puritan tradition generally, Holmes does not counsel a withdrawal from the world or a monastic sort of asceticism. What God has given, enjoy — and "be you content with your present condition." Meat is good, gluttony is not; drink is good, drunkenness is not; living in and with the world is good, yet attachment to and reliance upon the world is a costly and eternally damning sin. But the pervading mood of Holmes' letter to his children is that it is now up to them — and to God. "Although my care and counsel has been extended to you," now it is beyond my ken and control. Let your life be "squared" with the Scriptures; and be prepared, as courageous sons and daughters, to part with all else "for truth's sake."

A Letter to All My Children

MY DEAR CHILDREN,

A word or two unto you all who are near and dear unto me, and much on my heart as I draw near to my end and am not likely to see you nor speak to you at my departure. Wherefore I am moved to leave these lines for your consideration when I am gone and you shall see me no more. Take it as the real truth of my heart in love to you all. For as I have been a means to bring you into the world as corrupted and sinful creatures as you were when conceived and brought forth into the world (as so I was), even so are you by nature children of wrath as others are. And yet the Lord had mercy on me, and I trust He will show mercy on you, in and through the Lord Jesus Christ. As He has begun with some of you to cause them to know Him and to serve Him, to love and obey Him, so I trust He will show mercy to you all. Wherefore, my dear children, above all things in this world let it be your care to seek the Kingdom of Heaven and His righteousness first and above all things, and to consider what you are by nature — even enemies to God. Be you thoroughly convinced of that and, by actual transgressions, that you are sinners. Yet, know that such great love as cannot be expressed by man nor angels has the Lord sent and held forth: even his Son, his only Son, to save and deliver you from wrath. [By such great love you are] not to perish but to have eternal life, even to all and every one that believes in His only Son, for in Him is life.

And now my son, Joseph: Remember that Joseph of Arimathea was a good man and a disciple of Jesus; he was bold and went in boldly and asked for the body of Jesus, and buried it.

My son, John: Remember what a loving and beloved disciple he was.

My daughter, Hope: Consider what a grace of God hope is, and covet after that hope that will never be ashamed but has hope of eternal life and salvation of Jesus Christ.

My son, Obadiah: Consider that Obadiah was a servant of the Lord and tender in spirit, and in a troublesome time hid the prophets by fifty in a cave.

My son, Samuel: Remember Samuel was a chief prophet of the Lord, ready to hear his voice saying, "Speak, Lord, for thy servant heareth."

My daughter, Martha: Remember Martha, although she was encumbered with many things, yet she loved the Lord and was beloved of Him, for He loved Mary and Martha.

My daughter, Mary: Remember Mary who chose the better part that shall not be taken away and did hearken to the Lord's instructions.

My son, Jonathan: Remember how faithful and loving he was to David, that servant of the Lord.

My daughter, Lydia: Remember how Lydia's heart was

opened, her care borne, her spirit made to be willing to receive and obey the apostle in what the Lord required, and was baptized; and entertained and refreshed the servants of the Lord.

Now, my dear children, consider the great love the Lord has held forth in His Son, and [turn?] to Him for life and for cleansing and pardoning that you may be delivered from that great bondage and slavery that by nature you are in. Know you that it is the Lord only that must draw you by His own power unto His Son. The Son came to seek and save that which was lost, even to the sick — the whole need Him not. Therefore, be careful that you reject Him not. Defer not the present tender of grace, but while it is called day harden not your hearts; turn to the Lord in true repentance. Give credit to the Lord's own testimony concerning His Son, that is, to believe on Him and so shall you be saved.

My soul has been in great trouble for you, to see Christ formed in you by a thorough work of the Holy Spirit of the Lord that it may appear you are born again and ingrafted in the true vine; so you, being true branches, may bring forth fruit unto God and serve Him in your generation. Although my care and counsel has been extended to you, as you well know, yet it is the Lord who must work both to will and to do of His own good pleasure. Wherefore, wait on Him with care and diligence; carefully read the Scriptures and mind well what is therein contained for they testify of Him. Let your hearty desires be to Him that He would effectually be your Teacher by His Holy Spirit. Beware that you hearken to any that shall speak contrary to the Scripture, for if they do speak otherways it is because they have no might in them. Let your conversation and life be squared by the same, and they will direct you how to behave yourselves toward God and man.

Next to loving and fearing the Lord, have you a most dear and tender respect to your faithful, careful, tender-hearted, loving aged Mother. Show your duty in all things; honor her with high and cheerful love and respect, and then make sure you love one another. It has been my joy to see your love, one to another. Let it continue and increase, so may you be good examples to others. Visit one another as often as you can, and put one another in mind of the uncertainty of life and what need there is to prepare for death. Take counsel one of another and, if one see cause to advise or reprove, hearken to it and take it well.

Be you content with your present condition and portion God has given you. Make a good use of what you have by making use of it for your comfort [solace]. For meat, drink or apparel, it is the gift of God. Take care to live honestly, justly, quietly with love and peace among yourselves, your neighbors and, if possible, be at peace with all men. In what you can, do good to all men, especially to such as fear the Lord. Forget not to entertain strangers, according to your ability; if it be done in sincerity, it will be accepted, especially if to a disciple in the name of a disciple. Do to all men as you would have them do to you. Seek not honor or praise from men, but the honor that is of God by the truth: that is, part with all for truth's sake. If you would be Christ's disciples, you must know and consider that you must take up your cross and follow Him, through evil report and losses. But yet know, he that will lose his life for Him shall save it. If you put your hand to the plough, you must not turn or look back — remember Lot's wife; but, be constant to death, and you shall receive the crown of life.

Thus, my dear children, have I according to my measure, as is my duty, counselled you. May the good Lord give you understanding in all things and by His Holy Spirit convince, reprove and instruct and lead you into all truth as it is in Jesus. So that when you have done your work here, He may receive you to glory. Now the God of truth and peace be with you, unto Whom I commit this and you, even to Him be glory forever and ever, Amen.

(the 17th day, 10th month [December], 1675)

104

E. Testimony to the Church

WHEN IS A CHURCH A *BAPTIST* CHURCH? OBADIAH HOLMES ADDRESSES HIS letter simply to "the Church of Christ at Newport . . . who are baptized upon the professing of their faith. . . ." Letters from the Newport Church to the Boston Baptists often said merely, "To the Church of Christ gathered at Boston," while John Russell, the pastor of that church in 1680, described it as "a Church of Christ in Gospel Order." But gradually the word "baptized" became less a verb and more an adjective. In 1719 a letter from the Boston fellowship, which began "The Church of Christ in Boston Baptized Upon Profession of their Faith," was shortened that same year in a Newport letter to "We, the baptized Church of Christ meeting at Newport."[1] The distinguishing tag "Baptist," or earlier "Anabaptist," was meant — like most tags in the history of Christianity — to be a pejorative one thrust upon the despised sect by its enemies. The sect itself — like most new groups in the history of Christianity — saw no need for any label at all since it was only re-creating the true and pure church of Jesus and the apostles. But history is more powerful than logic, and denominational names are the result.

The church to which Holmes writes came into being more than a generation before. And though an informal fellowship may have existed in the late 1630s, the critical date for Baptist history in America (see p. 140, note 1) is 1644. John Comer, pastor of this church from 1725 to 1729 and the first one to take a serious interest in its history, wrote that John Clarke

> gathered and constituted a church, maintaining the doctrine of efficacious grace, and professing the baptizing of only visible believers upon personal profession by a total immersion in water. This was done, as near as can be gathered, about the year 1644, six years after the founding of the Colony; though the first certain record of this honored and religious action [is dated] October 12, 1648, at which time it consisted of 12 members in full and visible communion. . . .[2]

The twelve original members were John Clarke and his wife, Nathaniel West and his wife, Mark Lucar, William Vaughan, John Thorndon, John Peckham, Thomas and Joseph Clarke (brothers of John), William Weeden, and Mary Painter.

Membership had more than doubled by 1652, when Obadiah Holmes joined, along with John Crandall, Joseph Torrey, the black Baptist "Jack," and others. But the first major schism in 1656 (see above, pp. 44f.) reduced the membership back to around its original size of a dozen. Weakened by the further separation of Seventh Day observers in 1671, the church had only seventeen members when John Comer became its pastor in 1725. (During his four-year ministry, however, the number increased to 51.) Between Holmes' death in 1682 and John Comer's arrival in 1725, the church was often without a pastor. Richard Dingley was ordained over the church in 1689 but left for Columbia, South Carolina in 1694. William Peckham, one of the church's own elders, was finally elevated to the pastoral office in 1711. Ironically, following Dingley's departure, the church's membership (ten men, nine women) voted to place themselves for a time "under the ministry of the Rev. Mr. William Hiscox of the 7th day Church."[3] Jonathan Holmes, one of the nineteen members, voted for that move, presumably with appropriate apologies to the memory of his father.

When Obadiah Holmes served the church, its worship was simple and extemporaneous. More didactic than ecstatic, the service allowed for the congregation and minister to engage in extensive dialogue. And "prophesying" did not mean speaking in tongues or attempting to predict the future (Holmes specifically rejects "curious divinations"), but each member soberly explicating and applying a passage of scripture. Prayers, offered both by pastor and people, were unstructured, unread, *ex anima*. Baptism took place in a convenient mill pond and communion was observed "often." That communion was strict or "closed," only members of the church being invited to the Lord's table, and the singing of psalms was apparently shunned.[4] The earliest church covenant to survive is dated May 4, 1727; by that time the church had apparently relaxed some of its concern about worship with others. For the covenanters declared: "We promise not to retain a pharisaical spirit to withdraw in time of prayer, but to join with all such as, in the ground of charity, are true believers and churches of Christ."[5]

The style of Holmes' letter to "his dear and well beloved brethren" is consciously Pauline, both in its vocabulary and in the staccato of its imperatives. The flavor of Paul's letter to the Ephesians is clearly evident, for example, in the third paragraph of this letter. And, like Paul, Holmes mixes personal biography with professional counsel. His "tender love" arose from his long association with the church, which had already lasted a quarter of a century, with several years still to go. Yet he also writes with an awareness of their weaknesses — and of his own. Warning the church against exercising too much rigor in matters of discipline, he perhaps recalls his own adamant stance on more than one occasion. To all who would preach or pray or exhort, he counsels that they speak out of their own experience and not rely on the secondhand words of others. Indeed, much of Christian liberty and Baptist polity can be read in these words: "Try what you hear whether it is according to truth, and take nothing from any man until you have tried it and well digested it by a good understanding." Evil is to be opposed, to be sure, but not "in a cunning worldly wisdom of the flesh"; rather, fight evil "by the word of God through the help of His Holy Spirit of truth. . . ." Thus armed, you will gain the victory. The apostolic admonition to try or tests the spirits (I John 4:1) was no less necessary in seventeenth-century Rhode Island than it was in first-century Palestine: options were numerous and competition keen. We have seen in our day, wrote Holmes, all kinds of spirits seeking to deceive (even the elect!) "with signs and lying wonders." So, dearly beloved, "keep your feet sure upon the rock and your faith there, and the gates of hell shall not prevail." Wherefore, come, Lord Jesus.

To the Church

Unto his dear and well beloved brethren, the Church of Christ at Newport, on Rhode Island, who are baptized upon the professing of their faith, and continue in the apostles' doctrine, fellowship, breaking bread, and prayer.

DEAR AND WELL BELOVED
(FOR WHOM I HAVE EVER HAD RESPECT),

For truth's sake, I am in a manner constrained to write these lines unto you as my last farewell and as a true token of my constant love. The reason is [that I] find weakness upon me and may be removed suddenly and may be deprived of senses or memory, or may be by the enemy cut short of time as many are this day. * Some are taken away without giving any account of their estate with respect to eternity. Persuading myself that you will take well my affectionate desires for you, and what weakness you see in it [will] cover with a mantle of love, and [that you will] endeavor to make use of all you find in it that is according to God, so [let us] give glory to the Lord to Whom be all glory and praise, forever and ever, Amen.

My dear and well beloved in the Lord, I do judge it my duty to give you a short account of my present state with respect to my soul and spirit. My trust and confidence is only in the love and mercy of God, in and through Jesus Christ my Lord, who died for me that I might live in Him and to Him. And He rose again for my justification, even to justify all my weakness and aberrations; for in many things have I offended, but by His blood am I cleansed and by His death am I saved. He has brought my heart willingly to submit to death and rather to choose it than life. I am satisfied that the sting is taken away and that I shall inherit and possess a glorious eternity with Himself and Father and glorious angels and glorified saints forever.

The next thing is some words of my comfort and joy concerning you, or you that are indeed called, justified and sanctified. My joy is that you stand fast in the faith and order of our Lord Jesus. You shall also reap if you faint not; wait but a little while and the Lord will gather you to Himself — yea, where He is, you may be also. Therefore, I beseech you, as a brother in Christ, stand fast and faint not in tribulation, nor fear the face of men, but wait upon the Lord with patient minds, having your loins girt about you with truth. Let it be everyone's care and business to prove his own works. . . [several words missing]. For outward profession and form without power will not satisfy a sensible soul in the time of trouble. Yet, I tell you,

* These lines were written during the ravages of King Phillip's War; see above, pp. 62f.

108

faith will have fruits with it, both love and obedience with it, if it be true, lively faith. It will also purify the heart and life, holy and righteously, and that both towards God and man.

I beseech you also wait upon the Lord to see what talent or talents the Lord bestows on any of you, and put it not in a napkin but improve it for your Lord. Yes, how often have my fellow laborers called upon you to exercise the gifts you have received, and how it has rejoiced my soul to see my brethren come forth to profess in the church that, when the Lord removes us, you may not yet want any good gift nor will it much concern you.* Despise not the weakest gift, but cherish it. I beseech you that if any are or may be called into office to oversee the flock of Christ, take care of it and feed them with sound doctrines and good example in life and in a holy blameless conversation. Beware that you not bring into the church your own conceits concerning neither faith nor order, but what is according to the doctrines of Christ and the apostles. Condescend to them of low degree; say not to the foot, I have no need of thee. And rule with mildness, not with rigor. Instruct the ignorant, strengthen them that are weak, comfort the feeble-minded and — if any fall — be faithful, but not too rigorous (consider that you also may be tempted). God is merciful and may raise them up again; if they repent, forgive them.

I beseech you, brethren, beware that you envy not them that have obtained or received any gifts above another, but rather rejoice in the Lord. Let not the foot say to the head, I have no need of thee. Honor them that are in places, especially those that labor in the word and doctrine of Christ, those that are over you in the Lord and watch over yourselves as they that must give an account of their stewardship. I beseech you, consider one another to provoke one another to love and good works, and let not any man think of himself above what is meet [proper]. Be humble and lowly; be much with God in secret; try what you

---

* Yet, as noted in the introduction to this section, no one in the membership does step forward to accept the pastoral office when Obadiah Holmes dies.

hear whether it be according to truth, and take nothing from any man until you have tried it and well digested it by a good understanding. Often examine yourselves, and lean not to other men's judgments; beware of falls; endeavor and see that your evidence be good, which is alone the Spirit of God with your own spirit according to the Scriptures. Be much in holy meditation; read the Scriptures carefully. Beware of neglecting or slighting any ordinance of Christ; remember His death often, * but take heed lest you make an idol of men or ordinances.

If a little lad brings loaves of bread, despise it not. And be not too curious in searching or rather prying into one another's faults. Look into your own hearts and ways in secret. But when evil is plain, reprove it faithfully, yet with pity and grief, and grate [rub] not too much, for too much wringing of the nose may cause blood. † Make good improvement of your present season, whether liberty or restraint; always set the Lord before your face. Often consider your latter end, and be careful to keep yourselves pure and the members of your body, for both are redeemed. Keep your communion clear and distinct, and beware of partiality in all your designs among yourselves. Often beg of the Lord to send faithful laborers into His harvest and, if God prepare any, neglect not to send them out by prayer and fasting with laying on of hands. ‡ Discourage none that are fit, and preach the word in season and out of season. Sow your seed in the morning and neglect it not in the evening, not knowing which shall prosper. Have tender respect to the poor, and forget not to entertain strangers. Be not too royal, loving and friendly to all. Pity sinners; beseech, intreat, persuade them to be reconciled to the Lord — remember such were some of you. Give just offense neither to Jew or Gentile nor to the Church of

---

* That is, frequently observe the Lord's Supper or Communion.

† A line of Mark Lucar's which Holmes apparently borrowed — and took to heart; see above, p. 55.

‡ This is a laying on of hands for ordination to the ministry, not as a condition of full membership as among Six Principle Baptists.

God, and as much as in you lies, have the peace with all men. Do you to others as you would have men do to you. Love them that hate you, bless and curse not.

Try the spirits that are or may come forth, for every spirit is not of God. As you know, we have seen [much already] in our days, and I know there are worse spirits yet to come forth: I mean with greater power and all manner of deceitfulness, if it were possible to deceive the very elect with signs and lying wonders. [Such spirits] will take hold on many, to the grief of the upright in heart, but [this temptation] shall be to the making manifest of them that are upright. Keep your way to the mark that is before you, and keep your feet sure upon the rock and your faith there, and the gates of hell shall not prevail. Remember the good experience we have had of preservation hitherto — the poor weak ones, while tall cedars have been shaken and fallen to our grief and their wounding. So that you may stand, get out of your own strength and wisdom, and highly esteem the counsel and wisdom of God in the Holy Scriptures, and pray to the Lord to preserve you and to deliver you from evil. Beware that you do not strive to oppose evil in a cunning worldly wisdom of the flesh, but by the word of God through the help of His Holy Spirit of truth — against that, the Adversary cannot gainsay.

Contend for the faith of the Gospel with meekness, yet boldly and constantly witness to the truth to death. And break not the truth: declare it with reverence and in the fear and name of the Lord. Yea, be considerate and ponder your words and well understand your speech. Study plainness, and not curious divinations or words and sentences. Rather preach your own experiences than other men's words or works. And if God come in to help you, take heed that you not be lifted up with high conceits of pride and vain glory. Let the Lord alone be advanced, lest you glory in flesh and so lose your reward. Let nothing below the Lord satisfy your souls and spirits; covet not men's silver or gold; be content with your own condition and portion; envy no man's condition, whether greater in gifts or estate. In a day of peace or prosperity, boast not too much; in a day of adversity, then consider and bear patiently the chastising of the Lord, and wait on Him for your deliverance. Murmur not at His hand, but know that deliverance will come in His own way and at His appointed time. In nothing be careful [anxious], but make your request to Him: He cares for you. Often, think on that word of His, He will not leave you nor forsake you, and all things shall work together for good to them that love and fear the Lord, who are called according to the purpose of His grace. * Beware of covetousness and especially of hypocrisy when you are about any spiritual service, and have a careful watch one over another for good and not for evil.

These things have I written in tender love to you all. That is, I have labored among you this twenty-four years, and have not fainted, so I leave this as a token of my love. At last, though I die, yet my love and care to you do remain with you, and I commit this and you to the Lord. If any receive any comfort or counsel from it, give the praise only to the Lord who works the will and the deed only of His good pleasure and will accept His own work. Thus, I commit you to the Lord and to the word of His grace, to settle, comfort and establish you in the truth as it is in Jesus. And [for the] rest, I am your servant while I am in the body waiting for my change to be ever with my Lord in that glory He has prepared to give to them that love Him and wait for His appearance. Wherefore, come Lord Jesus, come quickly, Amen. Amen, says my spirit, even so be it, Amen.

* See Joshua 1:5 and Romans 8:28.

112

F. Testimony to the World

SHOULD ANYONE ASK WHAT CONSTITUTES "EVANGELICAL PREACHING," LET him read on. A popular nineteenth-century hymn, "Tell Me the Old, Old Story," epitomizes the basic material of Holmes' sermons. The pulpit is not a fountain for baptizing current events, nor is theological novelty the consuming passion. One has the impression that over and over again Obadiah Holmes presents "to your consideration a matter of great worth," namely, that "the Lord has had pity on poor sinners and does not desire their death but rather that they might live and be saved. For that end has God appointed a way, a new and living way by which you may be saved. . . ." This is the message, the gospel, delivered with studied plainness, drawn from Scripture and reinforced by experience. "You must be born again, and converted, and the old man must be mortified and you renewed. . . ."

Holmes' preaching or witnessing is often private, as he indicates below: at weddings, at funerals, on the military training grounds found in every New England town and village, and in private homes. All of this is done freely, not for pay, as Holmes states again here. And he draws repeatedly from those two wells that never run dry: his own memories of how God has dealt with him, and biblical history, prophecy, song, law, epigram, and instruction. The Bible that Holmes knew in England was almost certainly the Geneva Bible, first published in 1560. (John Clarke's Bible, which still survives, is a Geneva Bible.) The Geneva Bible was enormously popular among English-speaking Puritans or Separatists, both before the King James Version appeared in 1611 and for a half-century or more thereafter.[1] In England it was the Bible not of the churches but of the people. In New England, the Geneva Bible was read both from the pulpit and at the hearth. The Calvinism in its marginal notes was fully congenial to the theologi-

113

cal orientation of the majority, those notes providing immediately useful material for sermons and essential background for exposition by the members of the congregation. Many later editions had numerous aids to worship and to study bound directly with the biblical text itself,[2] so that even the ordinary man or woman, the "poor ambassador," could expound with some confidence and within a frame of common understanding.

In his "Testimony to the World," Holmes categorizes various types of sinners: the open, the secret, the moral, the Pharisaical, and so on. A point of major emphasis is that civility cannot be equated with Christianity, in illustration of which he draws a marvelous caricature of the respectable sinner. One suspects that it is adherents of the "New England way" whom he has chiefly in mind.

> One says, I have hated sin ever since I was born and heard of sin by instruction of my godly parents; not only that, but I am in covenant with God by their fatherly holiness and was baptized into their faith. . . . I pay every man his due, and also fast and pray when authorities have cause to command it. As for my faith, it is as my father or mother instructed us.

What could be more reasonable, more civil and polite, more deluding and damning? Opponents of the Half-Way Covenant could not ridicule more trenchantly than this.

There is simply no substitute for conversion — not works, not righteousness, not education, not worthy ancestry, not good repute among men. Only a single way remains, and Holmes describes it again. "Your work is only and alone to accept the proffer of free grace in and through Jesus Christ, and to be converted: that is, truly turned to the Lord both in heart and conversation [life], old things being done away and all things become new." What one must do, Holmes declared, is convince the sinner to love liberty, for it is "the love of liberty that must free the soul. . . ."

As noted in the Introduction to Part II, the manuscript of this last section of Holmes' Testimony is mutilated and his final words are lost. From the context it is clear that other sins were still to be condemned, other sinners were yet to be entreated. Nevertheless, it is perhaps fitting that Obadiah Holmes' testimony to the world remain unfinished. The outline — in fact, the details as well — of the evangelical story have already been made clear. And one can readily conceive of Holmes' determination and delight in telling that story again and again.

To the World

A LETTER UNTO THE WORLD, OR SOME CONSIDERATIONS
that are in my heart proceeding from my entire love to the sons of
men that are yet uncalled, lying in a natural state and are
enemies to God and their own souls by evil works. I say, my
love and pity is to them and my prayers have been for them that
they may be called and saved and delivered out of the snare and
captivity of Satan and brought into the liberty of the sons of
God. [I pray that] by true faith and repentance they might
manifest that their hearts were turned to the Lord by a conversion of holiness and righteousness both towards God and man.
[I also pray] that it might appear to be the true effect of faith in
the Lord Jesus Christ that they were turned from darkness to
light and from the power of Satan unto the ever living God who
desires not the death of a sinner but rather that he should turn
and live. Although by nature all are sinners, yet there are some
that are more openly wicked, others more secret, and others that
do deceive themselves by taking moral education and civility for
Christianity — and yet are not effectually called nor turned to
the Lord. Therefore, I shall manifest my love to each of these in
plainness and faithfulness to you at my last, even at death, as I
have done to you at my life upon all occasions when I could meet
with assemblies, either public or private, so that I might clear
myself from the blood of all men.

[1. Open Sinners.]

Now unto they or you that are so bold or so presumptuous
open sinners that are not ashamed of your evil ways and works,
but will commit your wickedness before the sun and neither fear
God nor reverence man, know that your sins go before to
judgment. It is a fearful thing to fall into the hands of the living
God who is a consuming fire and will recompense every man

according to his works. Without repentance you will be tormented with the devil and his angels forever, where the worm dies not, nor the fire ever goes out. The consideration thereof might make your heart tremble were it not hardened by Satan and the deceitfulness of sin. Or do you never consider that such open wickedness is often punished by the just hand of God in this life by the hand of men, even as it is written: The wicked shall not live out half their days. * You are commonly such as are not ashamed of your beastly actions as common swearing, cursing sometimes yourselves and sometimes the creatures you make use of by most terrible words and expressions, as also by open shameful drinking to the highest excess of drunkenness, to the great abuse of yourselves and others. Then are you fit to pleasure Satan in doing what he pleases to put into your corrupted hearts. Thence come quarrelings, fightings, murders and such like. As for uncleanness or wickedness of that kind, you endanger not only yourself to be wicked in committing it, but you draw others into the like practices and you glory in the same. It often appears among vain company, though your action may not be so evil in itself, that you do so glory and boast about what you have done and what you can do, never considering that it is your shame and that you must come to judgment. As the Lord says, There is no peace to the wicked. † So long as you continue in that state, you may expect nothing but fierce indignations of the Lord and, as you are an enemy to Him, He is your enemy. It is a fearful thing to fall into His hand, He who will be to thee as a consuming fire, if you repent not. What? Shall I speak peace to you in this, your present state and condition? No, no poor soul. You have no conceit of peace in the willful wicked estate you are now in, except you repent.

Yet, I shall present to your consideration a matter of great worth. That is, although you are in a very sad condition, yet there may be hope, for the Lord has had pity on poor sinners

* See Psalms 55:23.
† See Isaiah 57:21.

and does not desire their death but rather that they might live and be saved. For that end has God appointed a way, a new way and living way by which you may be saved: namely, the Lord Jesus Christ, and in His love unto the world has God sent Him that whosoever believes in Him should not perish but have everlasting life.* That blood is sufficient to cleanse you and make you as white as wool or snow, though your sins were as scarlet and bloody. Therefore, when Satan tells you that there is no hope for you, it is a lie, for he has been a liar from the beginning. Although you are the worst of men and chief of sinners, yet such have others been that have found mercy at the hands of the Lord — and I am not altogether unacquainted with your condition.†

Although you are hardened by the deceitfulness of sin, yet remember what checks of conscience you have had many times: either when some shame was likely to befall you among men, or some sudden accident or stroke from the Lord, or some sickness that death looked you in the face. Oh! then, how did your strong heart fail you and your conscience accuse you and gnaw like a worm or rather torment you! And your wicked companions fled far from you and despair approached. How near to some speedy execution were you in your own mind when your sins were plain before you, as though they were written in a book. Yea, it may be that being so clear before you, you thought others saw them also. Oh, poor soul, remember what you promised: if but once more delivered from shame or danger, you would become another man! But alas, alas, no sooner delivered, but all forgotten!

But I tell you, all your sins can no way be removed or forgiven but by the Lord Himself in laying your iniquity upon His dear Son. This is the condemnation, that Christ the true

* See John 3:16, the most familiar and frequently used verse of scripture in the evangelical repertoire.
† This is "experimental preaching"; here, and in the paragraph that follows, Holmes recalls his own time of life as an "open sinner."

117

light is come into the world, and yet men love darkness rather than light because their deeds are evil.* Wherefore, I beseech you, despise not this light since the Lord, in love, sent Him into the world to save poor fallen man. And the Father only requires you to accept Him by believing in Him for life, for He will in no way cast off them that are given of the Father and come to Him. I do not say that you have been such and such a sinner and, therefore, are unmeet or are unworthy; for, I tell you, the Lord is gracious and merciful, pardoning iniquity, transgressions and sin. Only consider, that if you come to Him, you must forsake all for Him, and not think to return to your evil ways. For you must be born again, and converted, and the old man must be mortified and you renewed in the spirit of your mind, accepting the grace and mercy tendered. For there is no other name under heaven by which man can be saved but by the Lord Jesus Christ.† This I have often declared among you, poor sinners, in most tender love to your souls and in true love to my Lord, taking all occasions as may present themselves to preach the word to you both in season and out, both in the public and more private assemblies (such as trainings, marriages, burials and from house to house), and that not without some danger. Neither did I ever covet or desire your estate, but your soul's welfare — the Lord only knows.

I could boldly say that I could freely spend or be spent for the love I have to poor sinners, though I hate your sin and must ever witness against all sin, both in myself and in others. That is why I have been carried out to speak often to you, because the Lord has shown mercy to me who was a child of wrath as much as others. And by grace am I saved by faith: it is the gift of God.‡ Therefore, I leave this for you as a true token of my love. If you receive it in love, it may be profitable for you; or, if you make a mockery of it or scorn and reject counsel, it is against

* See John 3:19.
† See Acts 4:12.
‡ See Ephesians 2:8.

118

your own soul. I have discharged my duty unto you all and leave you to the Lord, and I shall give up my account with joy that I have been faithful in a little and shall receive my reward from the Lord.

[2. Secret Sinners.]

Now unto you that are not so openly bold sinners as [act] shamelessly before the sun but are more secret in their actings of their wicked works: you are ready to blame the former sort, although you are in the evil state of nature and are as much given up to wicked works as the others. But you endeavor [seek] privacy and secrecy and commonly take the secret places and times, as in the night season, to commit these wickednesses. In the dark, these sinners are often thinking and saying, None sees. None shall know the thing they do or would commit if not by the sight of man prevented. These men or women are commonly not so outwardly boastful before men as the former sort, yet wicked in their minds, though they carry it secretly as to outward appearances before men. I have somewhat to say to you, which thing take in love as I truly tender it to you. It may be you will not curse me to my face, as when I have formerly spoken to you in such conditions. Nor will you say much against me; yet I question not but that you secretly hate to be reformed and will count me your enemy for telling you the truth. Yet, know you that your condition is dangerous and that without repentance you shall be turned into hell, among that condemned and damned party, as a just sentence from the Lord. As He said, Depart from me, you workers of iniquity; for, although you did your evil deeds in secret, yet I say all your works, yea, the imaginations of your heart [are evil]. And because I did not discover your secret works nor speedily punish them, you thought I was [favorable] to you, but I will set your sins before your face and will give you your reward, except you repent and accept my proffer of my favor which I tender to all men, even of my beloved Son whom I have sent to save the sinner.*

* See Psalms 6:8; Genesis 6:5; and Romans 2:16.

Now I entreat you, sit down and ponder a little on your condition. Consider your ways, all you that forget God and think He sees not or will not call you to account. Oh, that you will but understand that the Lord Omnipotent is present in all places at all times, even while your evil thought and imaginations and secret contrivances are to effect your wicked and evil actions. Commonly, you secret sinners are given over to all manner of evil, only you would not have it so appear to men — except it be to such companions in secret wickedness as yourselves. That is the reason you take pains to accomplish your evil purposes in dark times, lest your deeds might be discovered. Therefore, commonly you take the night for your purposes, for you cannot rest until you have brought it forth. And commonly your works in lying, swearing, and filthy communication among one another with reproachful speeches against the truth and the professor thereof [make others] think it strange that they run not with you to the same excess of riot with yourselves. Then is your time to drink and be drunk, abuse yourselves and one another. Then is your time to take to game cards and wickedly sport yourselves. Then is your time to attempt and act uncleanness — all of which you labor to keep from men that are civil, or that may punish you for such evil deeds. Yea, it is a shame to speak of what is done by you in secret. And yet, that holy, righteous and just God sees, [and He] will judge with righteous judgment.

Oh, my heart is troubled for you; my bowels have often yearned toward you in pity to your soul's estate. I have often spoken, and now I do leave this as a true token of my love to you. Therefore, even before you, I shall give you a word of counsel. And that is not to continue in evil but speedily to return to the Lord by true repentance, by confession and forsaking, and then you shall find mercy. For the Lord is full of mercy and full of compassion; therefore, while it is called day, harden not your hearts. The Father of mercy has in mercy sent his only Son into the world to save poor sinners that come to Him for life, not

120

only to save from judgment but from the power of sin, that sin should not reign in our mortal bodies. Therefore, consider the love of the Lord; beware of rejecting the counsel of God against yourselves. Neglect not when any man preach so as to suit your case, and neglect not the public assembly where Christ is preached. For the Lord has appointed that way and means for the ordinary begetting of faith, by which means He accompanies His Holy Spirit to open the hearts of men and women. [One sees first] their miserable condition by nature, then God's free grace held out by Jesus Christ. So give diligent heed to what is spoken and receive the counsel of the Lord to go alone unto Christ for life and salvation, and to Him alone.

I am wholly insensible [unaware] of your sad condition, and it may be at some times that the good Spirit of the Lord convinces you of sin, of righteousness and judgment. Oh, then how perplexed you are, with fear and horror in your conscience! You see your ways tending to destruction. But alas, poor soul, how to break off the company and companions you know not. It may be that you are ready to leave your present place and go somewhere whither you are not known — so as to escape them. Yea, it may be to leave your country;* yea, it may be [you are] even brought to despair in yourself, concluding [that it is] better to die than to live. Who does so adds sin to sin and heaps up wrath against the day of God's heavy indignation to fall upon ungodly men. But yet, poor soul, consider that it is only the Lord's mercy that you have yet your life and that it is He alone who must draw you to His Son. Whoever they be that do come to Him, He will in no ways cast away. No, none shall pluck them out of His Father's hand: He is greater than all, for He and the Father are one. Therefore, go to Him, for in Him is safety, and He is able to open your blind eyes and deaf ears, and to give you strength to forsake your evil ways and companies. And in a little time, you shall see all lovers will be as

---

* This, too, may be autobiographical, suggesting one of Holmes' motives for emigration.

strangers to you. Yea, they will as much hate you when you turn from them as ever they seemed to love you before. They will hate you much more if you turn away from their company and practices. But if God effectually turns you to Himself, then you will hate your own and their evils. Yet you will love their persons and be ready to tell them what God has done for you. And though your sin will be before you and upon you as a heavy burden, yet the Lord invites you to come to Him, and He has promised to give you rest. Believing in Him, you shall have everlasting peace through the Prince of Peace, the Lord Jesus Christ. Wherefore, seek Him while He may be found, call upon Him while He is near.* Arise and tarry not until you have found Him that is able to save to the uttermost.

[3. Moral and Civil Sinners.]

Now there is a third sort of men and women that seem to abhor and loathe the practices of the two former: the open, bold, highhanded sinners; and the secret ways of men that are done in secret. Yet, poor souls, they have little or rather nothing as an effectual work upon their souls, making but a fair show outward (like whited tombs), but alas nothing within but rottenness. And they are commonly of two or three sorts.

The first is the moral or civil man who is only satisfied with himself, saying: I do not lie or swear or keep wicked company as I see others do; I was brought up civilly and never was accustomed to such practices. Yet, all this while, [such men] never understood the true state of their own hearts as by nature, nor the loathsomeness of sin as sin, being the breach of God's holy law and contrary to His holiness. I must plainly tell you that your condition is not safe for you to rest quiet in. For except you be converted and born again, you can never enter into the Kingdom of God.† And if you have not faith, you can neither please Him nor be saved, for he that believeth not shall be

* See Isaiah 55:6.
† See John 3:3.

damned.* Wherefore, my counsel to you is to search your heart, try your ways, and return to the Lord. Rest not in that estate of your civility or morality, but hearken to the Lord in all His movings and stirrings which I am confident He many times causes, yea, and again calls. But men will not give the hearing, either pleasing themselves in their foolish imaginations of their deceitful hearts and foolish heads and brains and are wise in their own conceits, or else hearkening to the enemy, Satan, who tells them there is yet time enough to repent. And so the pleasures of this life, or the deceitfulness of riches, choke the seed. Instead of the good seed, the enemy sows tares, and so the poor soul lies in the snare of the wicked one who keeps the soul in bondage at his own pleasure. And the poor man will not hear: let the charmer charm never so wisely.

You will quickly tell me (in your hearts, if not in words), What [business] has any man to meddle with my estate? It is true: you stand or fall as your own master. Yet, I tell you, they that truly know the terrors of the Lord cannot but persuade you to turn to the Lord and entreat you to be reconciled to Him. I tell you that civility is not Christianity, although Christianity will work civility — and more than that. I speak now to all civil men and women to beware that you rest not on it to be your stay in a needful time. But come you plainly to search your hearts and way, and turn to the Lord, even to the Lord God, and to His love held forth to the world. Your work is only and alone to accept that proffer of free grace in and through Jesus Christ, and to be converted: that is, truly turned to the Lord both in heart and conversation [life], old things being done away and all things become new. [You then will] see your filthiness and sad condition, to be without God in this world, and [you will] see the unspeakable love of the Lord to set you free from the bondage of Satan and of your corrupt heart, and to open for you a fountain for you to wash in, even the blood of Christ.

* See Mark 16:16.

Beware that you trample not that blood under your feet, neither despise counsel, but consider those things that may concern your everlasting peace. Consider what I have said in love as truly I have tendered it, for I can say (as I have often said in your hearing) that I never coveted anything that was yours, only you. Having labored with care and diligence, and that with my own hands,* desiring rather to give than to receive and to owe nothing but love to any, [I would] improve that small talent the Lord has given me for His glory and the profit of others whom it might concern. I commit this to you as a token of my love, and I rest in peace in my soul and conscience as to the Lord and you and all men.

I have somewhat to say unto another sort of people or men who may well say that they abominate such things as are mentioned concerning the former people. Yea, it is well if they hate not these persons and selves too. I have had fears upon me that some do and to that end say, Stand farther off; I am holier than you. Now, these are commonly of two sorts.

One says, I have hated sin ever since I was born and heard of sin by instruction of my godly parents; not only that, but I am in covenant with God by their fatherly holiness and was baptized into their faith. And none can in any just way condemn me for wronging any. I pay every man his due, and also fast and pray when authorities have cause to command it. As for my faith, it is as my father or mother instructed us. We have read in the Scriptures to do to others as you would have men do to us, and that contains both the law and the prophets.

But my dear friends, this or more than this may be done by you, and yet you may be far from the Kingdom of Christ. Consider, did not the Pharisees do what you have done, or in that case at hand? And yet, by the Lord they were much condemned. Or do you think to say with them of old, We have Abraham for our father. For I tell you, even from hard-hearted

---

* Holmes makes explicit the point that he does not live off of his preaching, that he is not part of a "hireling ministry."

sinners among us Gentiles, God has raised up children unto Abraham. For you has He quickened those that were dead in trespasses and sins. You poor souls that cry up your righteousness! As I said before, how do you differ from them of whom the Lord pronounced, Woe be to you, scribes and Pharisees; you only make a fair show like to a painted sepulchre.* My care to you, and my advice to you, is to try yourselves by the Holy Scriptures, whether as yet you have ever seen your estate by nature even as dangerous and evil as the other. [You stand] without a true sense of a Savior which is only the Lord's mercy and love in laying your iniquity upon His only Son. See that you be in that new covenant of grace and peace through Him. [words missing] Then you will see plainly that there is no righteousness inherent in you nor done by you that either causes you to be accepted of God or that may give you any hopes of eternal life. Truly, as I have sometimes said, there is more hope for the messengers of God to convince the profane than the self-righteous man. And your self-righteousness — it does much to hinder you from coming to Christ. For as He says, The whole need not, but they that are sick,† and He complains that men will not come to Him for life.

Oh! therefore, beware lest you lose even that reward you expect and say that you wait for. Know that if you could keep the whole law (which you cannot), yet that would not save you. It is therefore the love of liberty that must free the soul: that is, the free covenant of God's grace and love towards us sinners, before we were [born]. It is then made out to us when we by faith do receive Him. And true faith is a working faith, manifest in yielding itself unto the Lord and also in works, not *for* life, but *having* life from the head distills itself into every faculty of the soul and members of the body. Truly, I have often thought about what the reason must be that either they come not into the obedience of the truth or why they are so easily drawn aside with

* See Matthew 23:27.
† See Matthew 9:12; Mark 2:17; and Luke 5:31.

the errors of the wicked or ways of mere men's inventing. And I conclude this is the main thing: men's high conceits of their seeming knowledge and their own righteousness, and also their not receiving the truth in the love of it, with some [mockery?] to the declarers and professors of it. [You also sin] in not bringing your deeds to the Scriptures to be tried by them, but either you are ignorant of them or, having some low esteem of them, sometimes take men's words only on trust without proving [testing] what is said in the Scriptures. And so you go on in things you profess, without either command or example from the Lord — and this only by the Father's testimony is to be heard.

My counsel is in love and fear of the Lord. Be careful to try your interest in Christ and take notice from the Lord [who] has tendered Him ever freely as a free gift of the Father to whole fallen man, that whosoever believes in Him should not perish but have even eternal life — in and by Him alone. Therefore, cast off all your filthy righteousness that you are ready to boast of lest men see your wickedness, and labor to see that your only way is to get that perfect righteousness of Christ upon you; although you be black, yet you may be comely through the comeliness of Christ. Give diligent attention to the Lord, speaking to you either in secret or when you hear the sound of the Gospel held forth unto you, though it be by any poor saint of the Lord who labors for your good. I shall rest only [while?] in the body I am yours to serve in the love and fear of the Lord. I, as a poor ambassador, beseech you to be reconciled unto the Lord.

* * * * *

G. Last Will and Inventory

OBADIAH HOLMES' LAST WILL WAS WRITTEN SOME SIX YEARS AFTER THE Testimony, while the inventory was, of course, drawn up shortly after his death in 1682.[1] Perhaps one-third or fewer of the adult males in New England, and a far smaller percentage of the women, drew up wills.[2] Yet there were many reasons for doing so, and a "grand estate" was not a necessary factor in the decision to make a will. One could write a will simply to save the survivors from minor troubles or quarrels: as John Clarke observed in his will, "being sensible of the inconveniences that may ensue in case I should not set my house in order. . . ."[3] One could use his will to make his case to the world, as did the New England merchant Robert Keayne,[4] or to present his testimony of God to men, as did Obadiah's brother Robert.[5] And one could give specific instructions or counsel similar to that which Obadiah Holmes offered separately in the Testimony. But the primary purpose, of course, was to carry out the wishes of the testator concerning his or her earthly goods and possessions.

To accomplish this last purpose, Obadiah Holmes drew up both a will and a deed of sale on April 9, 1681. The deed of sale was made to his son Jonathan, who was also named as executor of the will. By the terms of the sale, all of the family's farmland of one hundred acres ("more or less") — together with houses, outhouses, barns, sixty sheep, six cows, two oxen, and a mare — were conveyed to Jonathan for the price of £105 and ten shillings.[6] In return, Jonathan as executor was to pay out all the legacies stipulated in the will, at the rate of £20 per year, beginning with the oldest heir and proceeding to the youngest. Since the legacies amounted to almost £500, five times the value of the farm and its "appurtenances," it is clear that Jonathan assumed a major obligation. Perhaps the purchase price was adjusted to take into considera-

127

tion these long-term obligations. The provision that the bequests were to be paid in money or its equivalent suggests that the annual yield of the farm — wool, fruit, grain, etc. — would over a period of time make the payments to each heir possible. Nonetheless, the forty-one or more grandchildren (if all were still living) probably waited many years for their £10 — and their bibles.[7]

The inventory of Holmes' estate is notable chiefly for the modesty of possessions which it reveals. Apart from houses and lands sold to Jonathan, the entire estate amounted to a bit more than £28, about the value of eight or nine cows.[8] Why some items were exempt from the sale to Jonathan is not completely clear. Perhaps the two mares and the colt listed in the inventory were not considered as farm animals but as transportation. Also the "tavern" may refer primarily to the tools and toolhouses associated with Holmes' trade as a weaver and thus, again, not part of the farm. They could then be sold separately, as they probably were. From the inventory it is clear that Obadiah Holmes' wealth was in the land or, as he might have preferred to say, it was in the Lord.

Last Will

THESE ARE TO SIGNIFY THAT I, OBADIAH HOLMES OF Newport on Rhode Island, being at present through the goodness and mercy of my God of sound memory; and, being by daily intimations put in mind of the frailty and uncertainty of this present life, do therefore — for settling my estate in this world which it has pleased the Lord to bestow upon me — make and ordain this my Last Will and Testament in manner following, committing my spirit unto the Lord that gave it to me and my body to the earth from whence it was taken, in hope and expectation that it shall thence be raised at the resurrection of the just.

Imprimis [In the first place], I will that all my just debts which I owe unto any person be paid by my Executor, hereafter named, in convenient time after my decease.

Item. I give and bequeath unto my daughter, Mary Brown, five pounds in money or equivalent to money.

Item. I give and bequeath unto my daughter, Martha Odlin, ten pounds in the like pay.

Item. I give unto my daughter, Lydia Bowne, ten pounds.

Item. I give and bequeath unto my two grandchildren, the children of my daughter Hopestill Taylor, five pounds each; and if either of them decease, the survivor to have ten pounds.

Item. I give and bequeath unto my son, John Holmes, ten pounds.

Item. I give and bequeath unto my son, Obadiah Holmes, ten pounds.

Item. I give and bequeath unto my grandchildren, the children of my son Samuel Holmes, ten pounds to be paid unto them in equal portions.

All these portions by me bequeathed, my will is, shall be paid by my Executor in money or equivalent to money.

Item. I give and bequeath unto all my grandchildren now living ten pounds; and ten shillings in the like pay to be laid out to each of them — a bible.

Item. I give unto my grandchild, Martha Brown, ten pounds in the like pay.

All [of] which aforesaid legacies are to be paid by my Executor, hereafter named in manner here expressed: that is to say, the first payment to [be] paid within one year after the decease of my wife, Catherine Holmes, and twenty pounds a year until all the legacies be paid, and each to be paid according to the degree of age.

My will is and I do hereby appoint my son Jonathan Holmes my sole Executor, unto whom I have sold my land, housing, and stock for the performance of the same legacies above. And my will is that my Executor shall pay unto his mother, Catherine Holmes, if she survives and lives, the sum of twenty pounds in money or money pay for her to dispose of as she shall see cause.

Lastly, I do desire my loving friends, Mr. James Barker, Sr., Mr. Joseph Clarke, and Mr. Philip Smith, all of Newport, to be my overseers to see this my will truly performed. In witness whereof, I have hereunto set my hand and seal, this ninth day of April, 1681.

OBADIAH : HULLME [HOLMES]
[SEAL]

Signed, sealed and delivered
in the presence of
  Edward Thurston
  Weston Clarke

(Edward Thurston, Sr., and Weston Clark appeared before the Council [of Newport], December 4, 1682, and did upon their engagements [pledges] declare and own that they saw Obadiah Holmes, deceased, sign seal and deliver the above written will as his act and deed; and, at the time of his sealing hereof, he was in his perfect memory, according to the best of our understandings. Taken before the Council, as attested. Weston Clarke, Town Clerk.)

Final Inventory of
the Estate of
Obadiah Holmes

An Inventory of the Goods and Housekind of Obadiah Holmes Deceased the fifteenth day of October, Anno Domini, 1682

	pounds	shillings	pence
Pewter valued at fourteen shillings	00	14	00
Wooden vessels and barrells valued at fourteen shillings	00	14	00
Brass and iron ware, valued at £1, 8 s.	01	08	00
Tavern [workshop] and chains, valued at £1, 8 s.	01	08	00
Beds, with furniture belonging, valued £5	05	00	00
Old wheels, with a glass and a firepan	00	04	00
One saddle, bridle, and pillion [pad of cushion behind saddle] valued at 12 s.	00	12	00
One chest, valued at 4 s.	00	04	00
Wearing clothes, valued at £3	03	00	00
Books, valued at 8 s.	00	08	00
Two mares and one colt, valued at four pounds, ten shillings	04	10	00
Debt due, the sum of ten pounds	10	00	00
One hundred and five pounds, 10 s. (as it appears in the deed)	105	10	00
	28	02	00
	105	10	00
	133	12	00

The above goods and housekind valued by Elias Williams and Rowland Robinson, this sixth day of November, Anno Domini, 1682.

(The above written inventory is entered on record in the 81st page of the Council's Book No. 2, belonging to the Town of Newport. Mr. Weston Clarke, Town Clerk.)

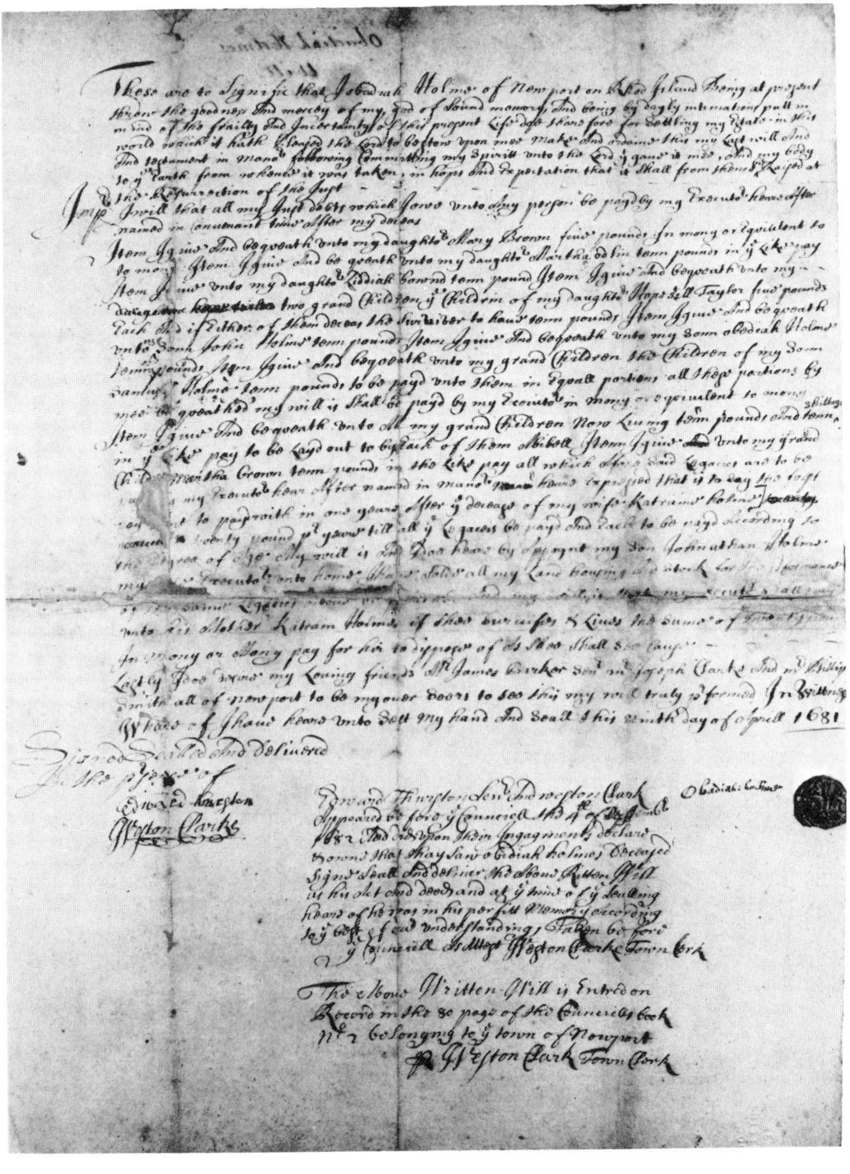

These are to signifie that I Obadiah Holmes of Newport on Rhod Island Being at present through the goodness and mercy of my God of sound memory, and being by dayly intimation put in mind of the frailty and uncertainty of this present life doe therefore for settling my estate in this world which it hath pleased the Lord to bestow upon mee Make and ordaine this my last will and testament in manner following Committing my spirit unto the Lord y^t gave it mee, and my body to ye earth from whence it was taken, in hope and expectation that it shall from thence be raysed at the resurrection of the just

Impr^s I will that all my just debts which I owe unto any person be payd by my Executo^r hereafter named in convenient time after my decease

Item I give and bequeath unto my daughter Mary Brown five pounds in mony or equivalent to mony. Item I give and bequeath unto my daughter Martha [illegible] ten pounds in ye like pay. Item I give unto my daughter Lydiah [illegible] ten pound. Item I give and bequeath unto my [illegible] two grand children ye children of my daughter Hopestill Taylor five pounds each and if either of them decease the survivor to have ten pounds. Item I give and bequeath unto my son John Holmes ten pounds. Item I give and bequeath unto my son Obadiah Holmes ten pounds. Item I give and bequeath unto my grand children the children of my son Samuel Holmes ten pounds to be payd unto them in equall portions all these portions by mee bequeathed my will is shall be payd by my Executo^r in mony or equivalent to mony. Item I give and bequeath unto all my grand children now living ten pounds and ten shillings in ye like pay to be layd out to buy each of them a Bible. Item I give unto my grand child Martha Brown ten pounds in the like pay all which above said legacies are to be [illegible] by my Executo^r hear after named in manner [illegible] expressed that is to say the first [illegible] to be payd within one yeare after ye decease of my wife Katrain Holmes [illegible] twenty pound p^r yeare till all ye legacies be payd and each to be payd according to the degree of age. My will is and I doe hereby appoint my son Jonathan Holmes my [illegible] Executo^r unto whom I [illegible] all my land housing and stock [illegible] [illegible] my Executo^r shall pay unto his mother Katrain Holmes [illegible] the sume of [illegible] in mony or mony pay for her to dispose of as shee shall see cause.

Lastly I doe desire my loving friends Mr James Barker sen^r m^r Joseph Clarke and m^r Phillip Smith all of Newport to be my overseers to see this my will truly performed. In witness whereof I have hereunto sett my hand and seall this ninth day of Aprill 1681

Signed Sealled and delivered in the p^r[illegible] of

Edward Thurston

Weston Clarke

Obadiah Holmes

Edward Thurston sen^r and weston Clark appeared before ye Councill the 4th of [illegible] 1682 and upon their engagements declared that they saw Obadiah Holmes deceased signe seall and deliver the above written will as his act and deed and at ye time of ye sealing thereof he was in his perfect memory according to ye best of their understanding. Taken before y^e Councill Attest Weston Clarke Town Clerk

The above written will is entred on Record in the 80 page of the Councills book N° 2 belonging to y^e town of Newport

p^r Weston Clark Town Clerk

Obadiah Holmes' handwritten will

Notes

Chapter 1

1. Quoted in Champlin Burrage, *The Early English Dissenters . . .* (Cambridge, 1912), II, 163.
2. Quoted in Perry Miller, *Roger Williams: His Contribution to the American Tradition* (New York, reprint 1962), p. 131.
3. See W. E. Axon, *Annals of Manchester* (Manchester, 1886), p. 59. The first enumeration of the population in Manchester, not until 1710, revealed a small town of only 8000 inhabitants; *Chetham Miscellanies,* LVII (1857), 41.
4. Quoted in R. C. Richardson, *Puritanism in North-west England: A regional study of the diocese of Chester to 1642* (Manchester, 1972), p. 5.
5. *Ibid.,* p. 11.
6. John Foxe, *Acts and Monuments [Book of Martyrs],* 4th ed. (London, 1887), VIII, 39-68; quotations are from pp. 62-63 and p. 53. For further information on Foxe's unique work and its enormous influence, see William Haller, *The Elect Nation* (New York, 1963).
7. Foxe, *Book of Martyrs,* VII, 143-287; quotations are from pp. 207 and 192. See the plaque erected in Bradford's memory in Manchester Cathedral.
8. Old Style dating, in which the New Year begins on March 25, prevailed in England until 1752, when the Julian calendar was finally adopted. The baptism of Obadiah Holmes on March 18, therefore, was in 1609 by Old Style dating but in 1610 according to modern reckoning. Here and throughout the book, all dates are given to conform to the modern calendar, i.e., with the New Year beginning on January 1.

   If Holmes was born about 1607 — and his own estimate is the principal source for that assumption (see Part II, Sect. A) — then it is somewhat unusual that he was not baptized until 1610. Illness, of course, could delay the baptism (Manchester was still recovering from a plague in 1605), as could the absence of a suitable clergyman. See J. Booker, *A History of the Ancient Paro-*

135

chial Chapel of Didsbury, Chetham Society, Old Series, XLII, 231-232; *Registers of the Church of St. James, Didsbury, 1561-1757,* Vol. I, part 1, p. 65.

9. Two brothers are clearly recorded as having attended Brasenose College, Oxford University: John, the eldest son (baptized May 3, 1607), admitted as *plebeius* in 1623 and matriculated Nov. 18, 1625; and Samuel, the third son (baptized, Feb. 23, 1617?), admitted as *plebeius* in 1632, matriculated Feb. 15, 1633, and graduated (B.A.), May 17, 1636. See *Brasenose College Register* (Oxford, 1909), I, 145, 164. Obadiah indicates that a third brother also attended Oxford, but here the record is less clear. A "James Holme" was admitted to Brasenose as *plebeius* on March 20, 1650. If "Jos." was misread or misrecorded as "Jas.," then this could be a reference (*Brasenose College Register,* I, 188) to Obadiah's youngest brother, Joseph. From the father's will (1640), it appears that some effort was made there to provide for Joseph's education when he came of age: "I give and bequeath to Joseph, my youthful son, forty pounds of current English money to be paid unto him. . . ." This bequest was by far the largest in the will; for further details of this will, see Part II, Sect. G.

10. In January 1616 glassmakers of Stockport began working "at a furnace at Houghton, just inside the Lancashire border, the site of which is still remembered by the name Glasshouse Fold"; T. C. Barker, *Pilkington Brothers and the Glass Industry* (London, 1960), p. 38. When Obadiah Holmes arrived in Salem, Massachusetts, he was given land "near to the glass house" in clear recognition of his trade and skill.

11. Henry Bettenson, ed., *Documents of the Christian Church* (New York, 1947), pp. 389-392. The Book of Sports was issued the following year, 1618.

12. Or like his younger contemporary, John Bunyan, Holmes may even have found a special delight in playing "tipcat." See Ola E. Winslow, *John Bunyan* (New York, 1961), pp. 48-49.

13. Henry Gee and W. J. Hardy, eds., *Documents Illustrative of English Church History* (London, 1914), pp. 528-532.

14. *New England Historical and Genealogical Register,* LXIV, 237-239.

15. Quoted in Richardson, *Puritanism in North-west England,* p. 39.

16. *Ibid.,* p. 10.

17. Preston was a major seaport in the seventeenth century, only later to be clearly outdistanced by its rival twenty-five miles to the south, Liverpool; Thomas Baines, *Lancashire and Cheshire, Past and Present . . .* (London, 1867?), I, 684.

18. James K. Hosmer, ed., *Winthrop's Journal* (New York, 1908), I, 274. Winthrop also observed: ". . . many ships arrived this year

[1638], with people of good quality and estate, notwithstanding the [Privy] council's order that none should come without the king's license; but God so wrought that some obtained license, and others came away without" (p. 271).

19. *Essex Institute Historical Collections* (hereafter *EIHC*), IV, 183-184; V, 168, 171, 219. On the early history of Salem, see Richard P. Gildrie, *Salem, Massachusetts, 1626-1683: A Covenant Community* (Charlottesville, Va., 1975).

20. For population estimates, see *EIHC*, XLII, 379; a careful calculation for 1637 placed the number of families in Salem at 226, the population at about 900. Concerning the glass factory where "small diamond window panes" were apparently made, see *EIHC*, XVI, 1-7. Holmes' co-workers were Ananias and John Conckline and Lawrence Southwick; Southwick and family achieved notoriety later as Quaker dissenters (see above, p. 50).

21. *EIHC*, V, 219; IX, 134; XXXVII, 101; G. F. Dow, *Records and Files of the Quarterly Courts of Essex County, Massachusetts* (Salem, 1911), I, 33, 74, 78, 85n.

22. When Roger Williams chided New England Congregationalists for refusing to separate cleanly from the Church of England, he called attention to the carefully cultivated ambiguity which the first-generation Puritans tried desperately to maintain: to be in the Church of England while creating a new and different "true church" of England, to be separated geographically but not theologically — or emotionally. Williams contended that it was impossible to have it both ways; one was either part of a corrupt establishment, or one forthrightly rejected and renounced it. On the views of Williams, often misunderstood and misinterpreted, see Perry Miller, *Roger Williams* (cited in n. 2 above), and Edmund S. Morgan, *Roger Williams: The Church and the State* (New York, 1967).

23. Williston Walker, *Creeds and Platforms of Congregationalism* (Boston, reprint 1960), pp. 117-118; *EIHC*, I, 37-39; and Richard D. Pierce, ed., *The Records of the First Church in Salem, Massachusetts, 1629-1736* (Salem, 1974), pp. 3-8.

24. *EIHC*, VI, 6.

25. Clearly, Obadiah Holmes had not yet come to Williams' position (which later was very much to be his own) that the civil magistrate should never meddle in ecclesiastical affairs. Fowler, perhaps more in humor than in wrath, remarked to Holmes that he (Fowler) had wet his bed and that the church — all too meddlesome in the minds of some — ought to take up that weighty matter at its next meeting. See *EIHC*, VIII, 125; G. F. Dow, *Records and Files*, I, 25.

26. Bowen, *Early Rehoboth* (Rehoboth, 1945-50), II, 134.

27. *EIHC*, IX, 137.

28. Joseph B. Felt, *The Ecclesiastical History of New England* . . . (Boston, 1855, 1862), I, 551; J. O. Austin, *The Genealogical Dictionary of Rhode Island* . . . (Baltimore, reprint 1969), pp. 103-104; and Francis Baylies, *An Historical Memoir of the Colony of New Plymouth* . . . (Boston, 1866), I, 200. Baylies states that the grant of land to Holmes was recorded March 28, 1645.

29. Austin, *loc. cit.* In Massachusetts at this time, a freeman took an oath of loyalty to the Commonwealth and its "wholesome laws," concluding his pledge in these words: "Moreover, I do solemnly bind myself in the sight of God that when I shall be called to give my voice touching any such matter of this state wherein freemen are to deal, I will give my vote and suffrage as I shall in my own conscience judge best to conduce and tend to the public weal of the Body, without respect of persons or favor of any man." See *Laws and Liberties of Massachusetts* (Cambridge, Mass. [reprint of the 1648 edition], 1929).

30. On this surveying team, see Allyn B. Forbes, ed., *Winthrop Papers,* V (Boston, 1947), 177-178. Both Rhoades and Carpenter, like Holmes, later became Baptists, though Carpenter soon fell away (Baylies, *New Plymouth,* I, 199, 201). On King Phillip's War, see above, pp. 62f.

31. For population estimates in Rehoboth, see Bowen, *Early Rehoboth,* I, 17-22; IV, 12.

32. William B. Sprague, *Annals of the American Pulpit* (New York, reprint 1969), I, 115-116.

33. Bowen, I, 29.

34. John Clarke, *Ill Newes from New-England: Or, a Narative of New-Englands Persecution* . . . (London, 1652); reprinted in *Collections of the Massachusetts Historical Society,* 4th Ser., II (Boston, 1854), 54. All page references to *Ill Newes* are to this later printing. The original is available on microfilm, American Culture Series, Roll 6, # 58 (Xerox-University Microfilm, Ann Arbor, Michigan).

35. Thomas Cobbet, *The Civil Magistrates Power in matters of Religion . . . Together with A brief Answer to a certain Slanderous Pamphlet called Ill Newes from New-England . . .* (London, 1653; facsimile reprint, New York, 1972, with original pagination). Quotation above is from pp. 49-50 of the appended "A brief Answer." For more on Cobbet, see above, pp. 36f.

36. *Ill Newes,* p. 53.

37. Cobbet, ". . . A brief Answer," pp. 48, 51.

38. *Winthrop's Journal,* II, 177. The term "Anabaptist," meaning rebaptizer, was applied by their enemies to those Christians

who regarded infant baptism as no baptism at all and therefore baptized only adults, or "believers." From the latter's point of view, this was the first valid baptism; from the point of view of infant baptizers, it was a second baptism and thus a wholly unacceptable repudiation of the first. On the gradual adoption of the "Baptist" label in America, see Part II, Sect. E.

39. Nathaniel B. Shurtleff, ed., *Records of the Governor and Company of the Massachusetts Bay in New England* (hereafter *Mass. Records*), II (Boston, 1853, 1854), 85.

40. *The Complete Writings of Roger Williams,* 7 vols. (New York, reprint 1963 [Vol. VII appears only in this edition]), VI, 188. Williams adds that he believes that this practice "comes nearer the first practice of our great Founder Christ Jesus than other practices of religion do"; nevertheless, he doubts the validity and authority of all churches or ministries beyond the apostolic age. See also his letter to John Winthrop, Jr., Feb. 24, 1650, in VI, 192.

41. See Burrage, *Early English Dissenters,* I, 322, 326, 366; II, 302-304, 316.

42. *Ill Newes,* p. 46.

43. See Part II, Sect. A.

44. Obadiah Holmes said that he "separated from their Assemblies," but Cobbet — though accusing him of being a schismatic — said that Holmes could not really separate himself from the church. Since he did not admit himself to the church, he could not withdraw himself from it: it was done by the brethren. ". . . as the bond was made with their consent, so with the same consent it must be loosed." Because of his pride, his censoriousness, his offensive attitude toward authority ("masterliness"), and his obstinate refusal to reform, "they cut him off"; "A brief Answer," p. 52. According to Francis Baylies (*New Plymouth*, I, 210), this was Plymouth Colony's "first schism."

45. *Mass. Records,* III, 173-174.

46. *Ill Newes,* pp. 46-47.

47. *Ibid.,* p. 47; Nathaniel B. Shurtleff, ed., *Records of the Colony of New Plymouth in New England* (hereafter *Plymouth Records*) (Boston, 1855), II, 147, 156.

48. *Plymouth Records,* II, 162.

49. See above, pp. 29-32. While Holmes was engaged in litigation in Rehoboth, a lawyer was trying to collect a debt for him back in Salem (June 27, 1650); Dow, *Records . . . of Essex County,* I, 194.

50. Cotton Mather, *Magnalia Christi Americana; or, The Ecclesiastical History of New England* (New York, reprint 1967), II, 520-521. The *Magnalia* was first published in 1702.

Notes

Chapter 2

1. The long contest between the Baptist churches in Newport and in Providence concerning which one was the earlier (1638 or 1639) seems largely beside the point. The critical date for Baptists in Rhode Island — and in America — was 1644 when a) the Newport church, a Calvinist body, became clearly a *baptizing* church; b) Williams' *Bloudy Tenent of Persecution* was published in London; c) Massachusetts resolved to make "Anabaptistry" illegal; and d) the "new baptism" that had swept the Calvinist Baptist churches in England was available for export to America. The London Confession of 1644 was probably of greater significance to English Baptist life than to American; nonetheless, after this date its moderate and rational tone helped to dissociate Baptists everywhere from the extravagant fanaticism of sixteenth-century continental Anabaptists.
2. Samuel Gorton (ca. 1592-1677), a native of the same Manchester area where Obadiah Holmes grew up — and for a time a weaver in London — came to Boston in 1637. Continuously harassed for his eccentric religious views, he went back to England in 1644, only to return to America in 1648 armed with a letter from the Earl of Warwick telling the Massachusetts authorities to leave him alone. He settled in Shawomet, Rhode Island, which town he promptly renamed Warwick.
3. On the origins of the Seventh-Day Baptist Church in Newport, see above, pp. 51-59.
4. Quoted from Backus' copy of the Record Book of the First Baptist Church, Newport; in Rhode Island Historical Society, Backus Papers, Vol. II, Folder 21, p. 17. Also see in the Newport Historical Society, Vault A, Box 50, Folder 5.
5. *Mass. Records,* III, 67-68. Witter died eight years after "the visit," at the age of 75; Alonzo Lewis and James R. Newhall, *History of Lynn . . .* (Lynn, 1890), pp. 130-131.
6. An even broader (or subtler) purpose is suggested by John G. Palfrey in his massive *History of New England,* 5 vols. (Boston, 1865-1890). In his discussion of the visit to Lynn (Vol. II, 350-354), Palfrey argues that the whole episode was a careful plot contrived by John Clarke to prove that Massachusetts was hostile to the interests of Rhode Islanders generally and to the inhabitants of Aquidneck Island particularly. In so doing, he would weaken the influence of his political competitor on the Island, William Coddington, who — rejecting the patent earlier secured by Roger Williams in 1644 — sought closer ties with and possibly even annexation by either Plymouth or Massachusetts Bay. If anyone was "plotting" to make much of this seemingly innocent visit, I do not believe that it was Clarke; see note 36,

140

below.) On the Clarke-Coddington dispute, see Dennis Allen O'Toole, "Exiles, Refugees, and Rogues: The Quest for Civil Order in . . . Providence Plantations, 1636-1654" (Ph. D. diss., Brown University, 1973).

7. *Ill Newes,* p. 28.

8. *Ibid.*

9. *Ibid.,* pp. 29-30.

10. Until 1639 only the General Court existed in Massachusetts, but then the Court of Assistants and the county courts came into being. County courts were empowered to deal with cases not involving divorce or banishment, or crimes against life and limb. The Court of Assistants could function in these lesser cases also; at the same time it served as a Court of Appeals. See Emory Washburn, *Sketches of the Judicial History of Massachusetts . . .* (Boston, 1840); George F. Dow, *Records and Files of the Quarterly Courts of Essex County, Massachusetts* (Salem, 1911), preface to Vol. I; and Wilfred O. Cross, "The Role and Status of the Unregenerate in the Massachusetts Bay Colony, 1629-1729" (Ph. D. diss., Columbia University, 1957).

11. *Ill Newes,* p. 32.

12. The General Court consisted of John Endicott (ca. 1589-1665), a citizen of Salem who was also Governor of the Bay Colony at this time and again from 1655 to 1664; Thomas Dudley (1576-1653), Deputy Governor in 1651 and in twelve other years — as well as governor in 1634, 1640, 1645, and 1650; Richard Bellingham (ca. 1592-1672), Governor of the Bay Colony the last seven years of his life in addition to holding that office in 1641 and 1654; William Hibbins (? -1654), an assistant in the General Court from 1643 to 1654, whose wife, Ann, was executed as a witch on June 19, 1656 (John Endicott signing the order); and Increase Nowell (1590-1655), who, like most of the others, was an original patentee of the Bay Colony, coming over on the *Arbella* with John Winthrop.

13. *Ill Newes,* pp. 33-34.

14. The title page of Clarke's treatise read:
Ill Newes from New-England: Or A Narative of New-Englands Persecution. Wherein is Declared That while old England is becoming new, New-England is become Old.
    Also four Proposals to the Honoured Parliament and Councel of State, touching the way to Propagate the Gospel of Christ (with small charge and great safety) both in Old England and New. Also four conclusions touching the faith and order of the Gospel of Christ out of his last Will and Testament, confirmed and justified. By John Clark Physician of Rode Island in America. London, Printed by Henry Hills living in Fleet-Yard next door to the Rose and Crown, in the year 1652.

Clarke's title was explicitly a take-off on (or put-down of) Edward Winslow (1595-1655), governor of Plymouth and later colonial agent for Massachusetts who wrote *Good Nevves from New-England: Or, A true Relation of things very remarkable at the Plantation of Plimouth in Nevv-England* ... (London, 1624). With respect to this dig at Winslow, Thomas Cobbet was not amused (pp. 45f. of his "Postscript" to *The Civil Magistrates Power*).

15. Thirty pounds was a sizable amount in New England in the 1650s, quite apart from the overall shortage of cash; for some, it represented a total annual wage, and for Obadiah Holmes, it was more than the value of his entire estate apart from lands and livestock (see Part II, Section G).

16. Holmes' letter to the British Baptists is published in *Ill Newes,* pp. 45-52. John Spilsbury (1593-ca. 1668) maintained his trade as a cobbler in Aldersgate along with his ministerial duties, while William Kiffin (1616-1701) subsequently became wealthy in the woolen trade. A. C. Underwood, *A History of the English Baptists* (London, 1947), p. 60.

17. Cobbet says that Wilson "only laid his hand softly and gently upon Holmes' shoulder," declaring "Thou goest away under the curse of the Lord" ("A brief Answer," p. 33).

18. The Boston market-place on Great Street (later King, now State) was an open-air market "where farmers, sailors, townspeople and visiting Indians jostled each other for decades." A Town House was constructed there in 1657, later to be replaced by what is now the old State House; Walter Muir Whitehill, *Boston: A Topographical History,* 2nd ed. (Cambridge, Mass., 1968), p. 9.

19. Whipping was not an uncommon punishment in Massachusetts, especially in the early years. The *Records of the Court of Assistants,* 3 vols. (Boston, 1901-28) reveal about one hundred cases of punishment by whipping between 1630 and 1644, though the number of instances sharply declined in the 1650s and 1660s. Whipping was specified for such crimes as stealing, cursing, assault, fornication, drunkenness, hunting on Sunday, and servants or apprentices fleeing from their masters. Both males and females were whipped. Often the number of strokes was not specified, the only distinction in the judgment being between "whipt" and "severely whipt." As in Holmes' case, however, the "Whipper" sometimes had no discretion. In 1636, for example, one Edward Woodley was sentenced "to be severely whipped 30 stripes" for attempted rape, swearing, and house-breaking; in addition, he was sentenced to a year in prison with a coarse diet

"and to wear a collar of iron." In that same year the court ordered Anthony Robinson, found guilty in three cases of fornication, to have "20 stripes sharply laid on."

Just as the "Whipper" was often left no discretion, so the court was obliged to operate within certain legal limits. A 1641 law explicitly declared that "no man shall be beaten with above forty stripes for one fact at one time," there being clear biblical precedent for such a limitation (Deut. 25:2, 3; II Cor. 11:24); see *Laws and Liberties of Massachusetts* (Cambridge, Mass., reprint 1929), p. 50. Clarke reported that Holmes had been beaten with 90 stripes (*Ill Newes*, p. 63), but that number is reached by multiplying the 30 strokes by the 3 cords of the whip. Cobbet's retort was that "our magistrates do not reckon according to his arithmetic" ("A brief Answer," p. 34). Massachusetts had no monopoly on whipping in the seventeenth century. In Newport (while Holmes was living there) John Willis received 15 stripes for being found guilty of fornication (*Rhode Island Court Records,* II [Providence, 1922], 56); the whipping took place May 9, 1667. See Edwin Powers, *Crime and Punishment in Early Massachusetts, 1620-1692* (Boston, 1966); also, Lawrence S. Early, "Endangered Innocent, Arrogant Queen: Images of New England in Controversies over Puritan Persecution, 1630-1730" (Ph. D. diss., University of North Carolina, Chapel Hill, 1975).

20. *Ill Newes,* pp. 56-58. On Spur, see also William G. McLoughlin, *New England Dissent,* I, 21; and Isaac Backus, *History of New England,* I, 195n.

21. Three months before his arrest in Boston, Hazel had written to his "cousin," Samuel Hubbard in Newport (June 23, 1651), from his home in Rehoboth: "It is ordered by the [Plymouth] Court that he whoso is absent from their meeting in public, or set[s] up any other meeting shall pay 10 shillings a person for every day." Hazel added that he hardly knew what to do — stay or flee — but asked Hubbard to "be private in what is written here." *Magazine of New England History,* I (1891), 178.

22. *Ill Newes,* pp. 60-62.

23. Holmes' letter to Endicott (September 12, 1651) is found in *Ill Newes,* pp. 53-55. The nudity charge against Baptists was an old one — intended to make the practice of immersion as scandalous as it was deemed ridiculous; like the early Christian's "kiss of peace," the ritual of immersion inspired the imagination of the opposition.

24. Cobbet, a friend neither to Holmes nor to the Baptists at large, apparently gave no credence to the adultery smear or to lurid

tales of naked baptism; in the context where it would most naturally be included, nothing is said (Cobbet, "A brief Answer," p. 39).

25. Williams (1603?-1683) is, of course, the best-known participant — from either side — in this drama. Exiled from Massachusetts in 1636 and founder of Providence shortly thereafter, he was briefly a Baptist. During most of his adult life, however, he avoided all institutional connection with religion, believing that no true Church of Christ was possible beyond the age of the apostles. His friendship with and interest in the Baptists continued, nonetheless, as the letter to Endicott demonstrates. He and Clarke worked closely together in London for the political security of Rhode Island; yet, Clarke wrote critically of those who hold "that the Church of Christ is now in the wilderness, and the time of its recovery is not yet" (*Ill Newes,* pp. 19-20). How much direct contact Holmes had with Williams is not clear, though he does in 1662 witness a deed of sale between a sachem and Williams (*Early Records of Providence,* V, 284-285; see also XIV, 84). And Holmes almost certainly attended the debate in Newport between Williams and the Quakers in August 1672; he apparently wrote to Williams urging publication (*Complete Writings,* VI, 362).

26. For the entire letter, see *Complete Writings,* VI, 214-228.

27. *Ibid.* See also a letter of Williams written to John Winthrop, Jr. that same August of 1651, in which Williams refers to Clarke's and Crandall's release from prison, but "Obadiah Holmes remains." From this and an earlier letter to Winthrop (December 24, 1649) it is obvious that Roger Williams followed the fortunes of Holmes with both interest and concern; *Complete Writings,* VI, 213; Massachusetts Historical Society *Collections,* XXXVI (1863), 277.

28. Thomas Hutchinson, *The History of the Colony and Province of Massachusetts-Bay,* 3 vols. (Cambridge, Mass., 1936), I, 165 (hereafter, *History*).

29. Thomas Hutchinson, *A Collection of Original Papers relative to the history of the Colony of Massachusetts-Bay* (Boston, 1769), p. 272 (hereafter, *Original Papers*).

30. Hutchinson, *History,* I, 164n.

31. Hutchinson, *Original Papers,* pp. 308-310. Clarke was still in London at the time; in fact, he remained there for twelve years in order to secure — ultimately from Charles II — Rhode Island's remarkably liberal charter (1663).

32. *Records of the Court of Assistants,* II, 9.

33. Hutchinson, *Original Papers,* pp. 401-402.

34. *Ibid.,* pp. 403-407. The old question — how could Puritans persecute when they themselves had fled from persecution? — is

coolly answered by Cotton: "We believe there is a vast difference between men's inventions and God's institutions. We fled from men's inventions, to which we else should have been compelled; we compel none to men's inventions" (p. 406). Cotton continued to advance his hoary argument (used against Roger Williams) that anyone who obstinately refused to be convinced by the rational logic of Bay authorities was himself responsible for whatever punishment may come: such a person sins against his own conscience. The heretic, "a man willfully obstinate," errs "not through want of light, or weakness of knowledge, but through strength of will. Whence also he is said to be condemned of himself, of his own conscience . . . he that submits not [to the fundamentals] after once, or twice admonition is condemned of himself" (*The Bloudy Tenent, Washed, And made white in the bloud of the Lambe* . . . [London, 1647; New York, reprint 1972], p. 29).

35. Published in London by R. Cotes for Andrew Crooke; quotations are from the preface. John Spilsbury was also singled out for attack by Praisegod Barebones in his *Defence of the Lawfulnesse of Baptizing Infants* . . . (London, 1645). In the preface, Barebones spoke of the two great persecutions of infants, one by Pharaoh and the other by Herod; now comes a third, "a sore persecution raised up, and with much bitterness prosecuted against this innocent part of the Church," namely, the attack on infant baptism.

36. Against Palfrey (see n. 6 above), I would argue that it was Cobbet rather than Clarke who eagerly sought the confrontation and the test of Massachusetts' 1645 law against Baptists. As noted in the text, Cobbet saw himself as New England's chief warrior against this "rotten error," and "detecting" was one of the tasks he was "not unwilling" to perform. We do not know who set the constables on their "search from house to house for certain erroneous persons," but it makes more sense that it was Cobbet rather than Bridges. Nor do we know why the constables should suggest to the arrested trio that they go to Cobbet's church on Sunday evening, where a public confrontation would be inevitable. Palfrey's argument seems only a historically more sophisticated version of the Cotton ploy; if we banish, whip, or hang, it must in some way be your fault, not ours.

That same ploy was used three-quarters of a century later by a justice of the peace in Norwich, Connecticut, when in July 1725 he ordered several dissenters to be whipped with ten stripes apiece. The justice, Joseph Backus, asserted that "in a Moral and Proper sense, they whipped their own backs. . . ." Besides the whipping was neither severe nor unmerciful, being administered by "a single cord without a knot in it" (*The Proc-*

lamation of the Honorable Joseph Jenks, Dep. Governour [Rhode Island], Answered . . . [Norwich, 1726], pp. 9-10). Jenckes had vigorously objected to the whipping, which recalled to his mind the whole unsavoury episode of 1651, when "Mr. Holmes was whipped thirty stripes, and in such an unmerciful manner that in many days, if not some weeks he could take no rest, but as he lay upon his knees and elbows, not being able to suffer any part of his body to touch the bed whereon he lay." This account, neither contemporary nor eyewitness, is found in Jenckes' unpublished response to Joseph Backus' *Proclamation . . . Answered,* in the Rhode Island Historical Society, Backus Papers, Vol. II, Folder 27, p. 20.

    For another rebuttal to Palfrey — at some length — see Henry Melville King, *A Summer Visit of Three Rhode Islanders to the Massachusetts Bay in 1651* (Providence, 1896), pp. 33f. King is responding, however, even more directly to Henry Martyn Dexter, *As to Roger Williams and His "Banishment" from the Massachusetts Plantation. With a few further words concerning the Baptists, the Quakers, and Religious Liberty* (Boston, 1876).

37. Cobbet, "A Brief Answer," p. 1
38. Soon thereafter to be published in London "by W. Wilson for Philemon Stephens at the Gilded Lion in Paul's Churchyard," and with the official approval, Feb. 7, 1653, of Obadiah Sedgwick, licenser of the press.
39. Edward Johnson, in his *Wonder-working Providence of Sion's Saviour in New England* (New York, reprint 1910), offers capsule characterizations of the "seven sectaries" in New England with whom one must "never make league." The sixth group are the Anabaptists, "who deny Civil Government to be proved of Christ." The others, delineated with equal neatness, are Gortonists, Papists, Familists, Seekers, Antinomians, and the Prelacy (p. 31).
40. Epistle Dedicatory (no pagination).
41. Cobbet, "A brief Answer," p. 1. All Cobbet quotations below are from this appendage to the treatise proper, *The Civil Magistrates Power. . . .*
42. *Ibid.,* p. 3.
43. *Ill Newes,* p. 37.
44. Cobbet, p. 15.
45. Cobbet, pp. 25-27.
46. Cobbet, pp. 40-42.
47. In a letter to John Rippon (August 19, 1791), in the Backus Collection, Andover Newton Theological Seminary; reprinted in Alvah Hovey, *A Memoir of the Life and Times of the Reverend Isaac Backus* (Boston, 1859), pp. 252-255.

Notes

Chapter 3

1. See Part II, Sect. E, for listing of the original members of the church.
2. Newport Historical Society, Roll of Members, First Baptist Church; Vault A, Box 50, Folder 5. Unfortunately, the church records tell us nothing further about this precursor of all black Baptists in America. His arrival in Newport may well have been by way of Barbados, since the town had begun a cattle trade with that island by 1649.
3. Full text of the charter may be found in John Russell Bartlett, ed., *Records of the Colony of Rhode Island* . . . (Providence, 1856-1865), II, 1-21. Upon his return to Rhode Island, John Clarke received the thanks of the General Court for "his great pains, labor, and travail with much faithfulness exercised for above twelve years in behalf of this colony . . ."; *ibid.,* I, 510.
4. In his *Journal,* Samuel Hubbard offered a rare insight into the cooperative ministry of the Newport church. Hubbard and his wife were baptized by John Clarke in 1648; then, "I and my wife had hands laid on us by Brother Torrey, October, 1652. Andrew Langworthy [son-in-law] was baptized by Brother Obadiah Holmes at the mill, October 6, 1652. Our daughter Ruth . . . was baptized at 12 years old by Brother Crandall November 12, 1652." Samuel Hubbard, *Journal* (Providence, typescript 1940), p. 9, in Brown University Library. A manuscript copy is in the Rhode Island Historical Society (Vault, m-Hu-2). In both cases, the *Journal* has been extracted, probably by Isaac Backus.
5. All quotations are from Roger Williams' *Hireling Ministry,* in *Complete Writings,* VII, 152-153, 163-164.
6. In the Backus Collection at Andover Newton Theological Seminary (letter is dated November 15, 1790); printed in Hovey, *A Memoir . . . Isaac Backus,* pp. 251-252. For a convincing if unedifying example of the legal horrors which occasionally trapped New England's "hireling ministry," see Thomas Cobbet's own incredibly involved litigation in Ipswich during much of 1657; Thomas Hutchinson, *Original Papers,* pp. 287-309.
7. The plat and deed for this 1658 transaction are in the Newport Historical Society, Vault A, Box 50, Folder 9, # 4 (with another copy in the Rhode Island Historical Society); Mark Lucar served as one of the witnesses.
8. A reference to Holmes as a weaver appears in the midst of the Seventh-Day controversy discussed in Chap. 3, p. 59. While it is virtually certain that Holmes learned his craft as glassmaker in Stockport (see Ch. 1 above), it is at least highly probable that he also was exposed in the Manchester area to the techniques of shearing, weaving, and dyeing. Lancashire was a center for the

147

woolen industry as early as the sixteenth century, when "the majority of woolen manufacturers were quite poor men who worked at home, assisted by the rest of the family, and who owned a loom and perhaps a spinning wheel. They were usually small scale farmers as well, and though poor, were completely independent"; Norman Lowe, *The Textile Industry in the Sixteenth Century* (Manchester, 1972), p. 20. At the time of Obadiah Holmes' death, his farm included some sixty sheep (see Part II, Sect. G).

9. See Part II, Sect. B.
10. The King James Version.
11. E. S. Gaustad, "New Light on the Six Principle Controversy . . .," *The Chronicle,* XII (1949), 183-186. See also Richard Knight, *History of the General or Six Principle Baptists in Europe and America* (Providence, 1827).
12. On this point, see Part II, Sect. B.
13. Hubbard is identified more fully above, p. 52. On the migration of some of the Holmes children to New York and New Jersey, see Part II, Sect. D.
14. *Rhode Island Court Records* (Providence, 1920), I, 45; this general Court of Trials was held in Newport in June 1658.
15. *Complete Writings,* VI, 293-297 (November 15, 1655); 299-304 (May 12, 1656). In the earlier letter to the General Court of Massachusetts, Williams also urged the Bay Colony to permit Rhode Islanders to buy arms necessary to defend themselves against the Indians. Your trade with us "is as great as with any in the country, and our dangers (being a frontier people to the barbarians) are greater than those of other colonies; and the ill consequences to yourselves would be not a few nor small . . . were we first massacred or mastered by them. I pray your equal and favorable reflection upon . . . your law which prohibits us to buy of you all means of our necessary defense of our lives and families. . . ." Williams noted that the Dutch had provided the Indians with arms and artillery "openly and horridly," adding that he "refused the gain of thousands by such a murderous trade" (p. 296).
16. John Russell, *A Brief Narrative of . . . a Church of Christ in Gospel Order in Boston . . .* (London, 1680), p. 1; reprinted in Nathan E. Wood, *History of the First Baptist Church in Boston,* (Philadelphia, 1899), pp. 149-172. Russell was pastor of this church for less than a year and a half (1679-1680), dying shortly after his *Narrative* was published. Five London Baptists wrote a preface to his brief account, among them William Kiffin and Hanserd Knollys. They noted that in old England "our Brethren of the Congregational way . . . do equally plead for our liberties as for their own." How strange, then, that the Congregational churches in New England "should exercise towards others the

like severity that themselves with so great hazard and hardship sought to avoid." This is especially so, considering that "the present molestation given to them [the Baptists] is merely for a supposed error in one point relating to the right subject of baptism, which hath been controverted amongst learned, judicious, holy and good men . . . ever since the Reformation. Upon such occasions, for one Protestant congregation to persecute another . . . seems much more unreasonable than all the cruelties of the Romish Church . . ." (preface, no pagination).

17. Wood, pp. 84-86.
18. William McLoughlin, *New England Dissent,* I, 51, 51n., 61.
19. Three letters of Holmes to Winthrop survive in the Winthrop Papers at the Massachusetts Historical Society (14:45, 14:46, 14:46). All from Rhode Island, they are dated June 29, 1660; August 17, 1667; and June 9, 1670. They were made available to me through the courtesy of Malcolm Freiberg and Marjorie Gutheim. Holmes and Winthrop might well have encountered each other during the years when both lived in Salem around 1639 and 1640. For a recent life of Winthrop (but without any attention to Holmes), see Robert C. Black, III, *The Younger John Winthrop* (New York, 1966).
20. Most of the debate, which was taken down in shorthand by Thomas Danforth, remained undeciphered until recently. See the full text, with an excellent introduction by William McLoughlin and Martha Whiting Davidson, in the Massachusetts Historical Society *Proceedings,* 76 (1964), 91-133.
21. On the convoluted subject of changing Congregational polity and theology concerning admission to the church, see Robert G. Pope, *The Half-Way Covenant: Church Membership in Puritan New England* (Princeton, 1969); Edmund S. Morgan, *Visible Saints: The History of a Puritan Idea* (New York, 1963); and Williston Walker's still indispensable *Creeds and Platforms of Congregationalism* (Boston, reprint 1960).
22. Even if not on terms of perfect neutrality. You come here, Cobbet told Goold, "not on even terms, but as a delinquent" (McLoughlin and Davidson, p. 110).
23. On the history of Noddles Island, see Edward R. Snow, *The Islands of Boston Harbor* (Andover, Mass., 1935); the "island" is now totally absorbed into East Boston.
24. The meeting house was built on Back Street (later Salem Street) at the edge of the mill pond, this location being chosen explicitly for the convenience of baptisms in the man-made body of water.
25. The letter from Goold, Turner and Farnum is in Wood, p. 82. The final quotation is from a letter by Edward Drinker, a prisoner himself in 1669-1670, pp. 93f. Drinker, a potter who served as a deacon in the Boston church from 1670 to 1685, wrote his letter to Newport on November 30, 1670. Also, Goold paid a personal

visit to Newport in 1671 in a time of their need, namely, the
Seventh-Day controversy.

26. Rufus Jones, *Quakers in the American Colonies* (New York, reprint 1962); quotations are from p. 76 and p. 80, but see all of Ch. 3.
27. *Ibid.*, pp. 67, 69, 77. One of the couple's children, Provided Southwick, was whipped along with other Quakers in Boston in 1659. Lawrence Southwick's will is in *Essex Institute Historical Collections,* I (1859), 94. See also the poem, "Cassandra Southwick," written by John Greenleaf Whittier in 1843.
28. Thomas Hutchinson, *Original Papers,* pp. 325-329.
29. The letter, dated March 25, 1669, is in Backus, *History of New England,* I, 314-315.
30. Quoted, *ibid.,* p. 315 (from *Magnalia*, II, 460-461).
31. *Magazine of New England History,* I (1891), 197-198.
32. Tacey and Samuel Hubbard had three daughters, all of whom married and in time presented their parents with twenty-eight grandchildren. Ruth married Robert Burdick, November 2, 1655, and settled in Westerly, near the Connecticut border; Rachel, who married Andrew Langworthy, November 3, 1658, continued to reside in Newport and was one of the five schismatics in 1671; Bethiah married Joseph Clarke, son of John Clarke's brother Joseph, November 16, 1664, and they also moved to Westerly. The Burdicks had eleven children, the Langworthys ten, and the Clarkes seven.
33. Hubbard, in a letter to the Bell Lane Seventh-Day Baptist Church, London, July 3, 1669, in the *Magazine of New England History,* II (1892), 59-60.
34. Most of Hubbard's letters that have been preserved are found in Vols. I and II of the *Magazine of New England History*; a large number have unfortunately been lost, along with the original *Journal.*
35. *Magazine of New England History,* II (1892), 60.
36. Newport Historical Society, Vault A, Box 50, Folder 3. See also the letter from the Boston church to Hiscox and the other sabbatarians urging forbearance and the avoidance of a "censorious spirit": "But may we not say we are all in the dark, and see and know but in part?" Wood, pp. 108-109.
37. *Magazine of New England History,* II (1892), 175-176. See also Roger Williams' letter to Hubbard, written late in 1672, explaining why he (Williams) rejected the seventh-day sabbath; *Complete Writings,* VI, 361-362.
38. All the lines from this extended debate are taken from "A Brief and faithful Relation of the Difference between those of this Church and those who withdrew their Communion from it, with the Causes and Reasons of the Same." This detailed account was probably written by Samuel Hubbard, a most interested ob-

server as well as inveterate letter-writer and note-taker.
Though "interested," Hubbard appears to give each side its due.
Probably written down immediately after each session, this
contemporary report was copied into the Record Book of the
First Baptist Church, Newport, pp. 137-153 — presumably by
John Comer. In the Newport Historical Society, Vault A, Box 50,
Folder 5.

39. On Giles Slocum, see above, pp. 60f.
40. Roger Baster (ca. 1621-1687), a bachelor, is described on his
Newport tombstone as a "blockmaker." Though Seventh-Day
Baptists never became a large denomination, they moved from
New England into New York and New Jersey, then across the
Midwest and finally to the Pacific Coast, founding along the way
such educational institutions as Alfred University in New York,
Milton College in Wisconsin, and Salem College in West Vir-
ginia. In 1975 they had a membership of over 5,000 in 73
churches. (*Yearbook of American and Canadian Churches, 1976*
[Nashville, 1976], p. 96.)
41. Roger Williams challenged George Fox to a debate, but that
challenge reached the latter only after he had left the colony.
Williams accused Fox of deliberately ducking the confrontation
("this old Fox thought it best to run for it" since "he knew that I
was furnished with artillery out of his own writings"), but this
seems unlikely. Three of Fox's aides (John Stubs, John Burnet,
and William Edmundson) picked up the gauntlet, however, as
Newport was chosen for the site to discuss the first seven of
fourteen propositions listed by Williams. With the debate
scheduled to begin on Friday, August 9, 1672, Roger Williams
— then about seventy years of age — rowed from Providence to
Newport, a distance of thirty miles: God "graciously assisted me
in rowing all day with my old bones so that I got to Newport
toward the midnight before the morning appointed." The debate, which was supposed to last one day, went on for three, with
"a very great congregation of high and low" in attendance. On
August 17, the final seven propositions were debated in Providence, and here — with the imposition of severe time limits — a
single day sufficed. Fox's major work, *The Great Mystery of the
Great Whore Unfolded* (London, 1659), carried an introductory
"epistle to the reader" by Edward Burrough. So when he wrote
up the report of this long debate, Roger Williams could not resist
calling it *George Fox Digg'd Out of His Burrowes* . . . (in *Complete Writings*, all of Vol. V; quotations are from the introduction
by J. Lewis Diman). And for the first time, a work of Roger
Williams was accepted for publication (1676) in Boston! Two
years later Fox responded with *A New-England Fire-Brand
Quenched* . . . (London, 1678). Naturally, each side concluded
that it had won.

42. For the earnest and extended effort to dissuade the Slocums, see the Record Book, First Baptist Church, Newport, pp. 181-191. Also see the Backus Papers at the Rhode Island Historical Society (Vol. II, Folder 21) for a long letter from Mary Greenwood, a member of the Newport church, to Joan Slocum, daughter of Giles, written immediately after the excommunication. Even after the event, Mary Greenwood was still trying to explain why the church did what it had to do and was still trying — if at all possible — to bring about some reconciliation.

43. See Part II, Sect. E. Holmes' theological rejection of Quakerism is clear from Section B of his Testimony, below, but what his personal relationships were with these early Newport Quakers remains something of a mystery.

44. See *Records of the Colony of Rhode Island,* I, 299, 326, 337, 394; *Early Records of Providence,* V, 284-285, XIV, 84-86; *Rhode Island Court Records,* I, 11, 15, 48; *Early Records of the Town of Portsmouth* (Providence, 1901), pp. 322, 425-426.

45. Hubbard, *Journal,* p. 10.

46. *Records of the Colony of Rhode Island,* II, 537. The conspicuous absence of Roger Williams from the list can be explained by the growing Quaker control in Rhode Island. As Williams became increasingly unpopular among the Quakers there, Massachusetts went so far as to invite Williams to take refuge among them during King Phillip's War, provided of course that he would keep silent regarding matters of religion (Massachusetts Archives, X, 233).

47. See Douglas E. Leach, *Flintlock and Tomahawk: New England in King Phillip's War* (New York, 1958); see also his article in *Rhode Island History,* XVIII (1959), 43-54.

48. Newport Historical Society, Vault A, Box 103, Folder 1, #1.

49. *Mass. Records,* V, 347 (dated in Boston, Feb. 15, 1682); for earlier dealings with the Baptists, see *Mass. Records,* IV, part 2, 290-291, 373-375, 413.

50. See Part II, Sect. G.

PART II

General Introduction.

1. After Backus' first volume in 1777 came a second in 1784 and a third in 1795. In 1804, Backus prepared an abridgment of his *History,* with some additional material on the Baptists outside New England. In 1871, David Weston edited the *History,* correct-

ing errors, modernizing some of the language, adding extensive notes and an index (published by the Backus Historical Society, Newton, Massachusetts; reprinted New York, 1969). All quotations from Backus' *History* are from the Weston edition. On the life of Backus, with a fascinating interpretation of his significance, see William McLoughlin, *Isaac Backus and the American Pietistic Tradition* (Boston, 1967). Specific quotation in the text is from Backus, I, 173; for Obadiah Holmes material therein, see pp. 173-176, and the long footnote, pp. 206-209.

2. Newport Historical Society, Vault A, Box 103, Folder 1, #1. Howland states his motivation for copying the Testimony in these words: "It being a natural wish to know all that we can of those persons who appeared on the stage of life and acted their parts and retired before we came on, especially if they lived in peculiar and trying times and were prominent characters, and as everything which will serve to let us into the feelings and views of those men who settled our country should be gathered and preserved, I have copied the following writings of Mr. Holmes. . . ."

3. See *New England Historical and Genealogical Register,* XXII (1868), 351; this notice, which speaks of the Howland manuscript as "an autograph volume," is clearly in error.

4. Presented by Mrs. Charles Bull, September 1, 1922 (Newport Historical Society, Vault A, Box 103, Folder 2). Mrs. Bull also presented the original will of Obadiah Holmes to the Society, presumably at the same time.

5. *Record and Files of the Quarterly Court of Essex County, Massachusetts* (Salem, 1911), I, 85. Here Holmes and John Barbour witness the will of "widow Margaret Pease of Salem"; Barbour signs his name, while Holmes gives his mark (January 1, 1645).

6. See Section G. Also see the inventory of the estate of Obadiah Holmes' brother Robert, which placed a value of eight shillings on "a table chare" and on a chest.

7. See Joseph Jenckes' reply to an attack upon him by Joseph Backus (grandfather of Isaac), a justice of the peace in Norwich, Connecticut. The thirty-one page Backus pamphlet, *The Proclamation of the Honorable Joseph Jenks . . . ,* was privately printed in 1726. Jenckes' response, never published, is in the Rhode Island Historical Society, Backus Papers, Vol. II, Folder 27; quotation is from p. 20.

8. See Roger Williams, *Complete Writings,* originally published by the Narragansett Club *Publications* in six volumes (Providence, 1866-1874), republished with a seventh volume and introduction by Perry Miller in 1963 (Russell & Russell, New York).

9. G. A. Moriarty, "The Education of Dr. John Clarke," *Rhode Island History,* XV: 2 (April 1956), 41f.

10. Colonial Papers, Interregnum, Entry Book, CIV, 219 (Aug. 3,

Notes

1655); in *Calendar of State Papers, Colonial Series, 1574-1660* (London, 1860), I, 427.

Section A.

1. See D. B. Shea, *Spiritual Autobiography in Early America* (Princeton, 1968). This is a sensitive, well-written treatment of Puritan and Quaker journals and autobiographies in the colonial period. See also Owen C. Watkins, *The Puritan Experience: Studies in Spiritual Autobiography* (New York, 1972).
2. John Bunyan, *Grace Abounding* . . . (Roger Sharrock, ed.; Oxford, 1962), pp. 3-4 (a few spellings modernized here and below). For a careful analysis of the Puritan theology of conversion, see Norman Pettit, *The Heart Prepared* (New Haven, 1966).
3. *Grace Abounding,* p. 62 (par. 198).
4. *Ibid.,* p. 37 (par. 118).
5. *Ibid.,* p. 72 (par. 230). See also the readable biography by Ola E. Winslow, *John Bunyan* (New York, 1961); this study has the added merit of being written by one thoroughly familiar with the colonial American scene.
6. For a good discussion of early Baptist views (British and American) concerning the covenant of faith, see William G. McLoughlin, *New England Dissent,* Vol. I, Ch. 2.

Section B.

1. Robert Holmes (1621-1697) was a member and elder in Gorton Chapel, being chosen as a leader when still a young man. He named one of his sons "Obadiah." See *New England Historical and Genealogical Register,* LXIV (1910), 239.
2. See William L. Lumpkin, *Baptist Confessions of Faith* (Philadelphia, 1959), pp. 143-191.
3. In Nathan E. Wood, *The History of the First Baptist Church in Boston, 1665-1899* (Philadelphia, 1899), pp. 65-66.
4. John Clarke's long "Testimony" in *Ill Newes* (pp. 70-113), though offered in the name of Clarke, Holmes, and John Crandall, appears to have had little discernible effect upon Holmes' own formulation of his mature faith.
5. This mode of reading "the prophets and the psalms" prevailed generally in New England Puritanism; see, for example, Samuel Mather, *Figures and Types of the Old Testament* (Dublin, 1683); and Thomas Taylor, *Christ Revealed: Or the Old Testament Types Explained* (London, 1635) — both cited in E. Brooks Holifield, *The Covenant Sealed* (New Haven, 1974), pp. 135-138.

6. Wood, p. 150.
7. John Comer, Record Book of the First Baptist Church, Newport; in the Newport Historical Society, Vault A, Box 50, Folder 5.

Section C.

1. Two recent studies of mortality rates in colonial New England suggest that traditional historians have exaggerated the high death rates, especially for the seventeenth century. Nevertheless, John Demos concluded for Plymouth Colony that one out of five women died in childbirth or from associated causes, and that infant mortality was around one in ten. See John Demos, *A Little Commonwealth: Family Life in Plymouth Colony* (New York, 1970), pp. 66, 131-132; and Philip Greven, Jr., *Four Generations: Population, Land, and Family in Colonial Andover* (Ithaca, 1970), pp. 27-28, 109-110, 195-196. Clarke, in contrast with Holmes, was married three times, both of his previous wives having died. Clarke's second wife, Jane Fletcher, died in childbirth in April 1672, and the daughter born at that time — Clarke's only offspring — also died soon thereafter.
2. Thomas Cobbet, *The Civil Magistrate* . . . (London, 1653), p. 48 of the postscript; *Plymouth Colony Records,* II, 162. The Salem records, which list Obadiah Holmes as "excommunict," are not contemporary records but come from a book which the church drew up in 1660. "Into it were copied such earlier records as had been directed by the church vote." The importance of this is that many historians have been misled into stating that Holmes left Salem for Rehoboth as an excommunicant. This is quite unlikely. What is more likely is that the church in 1660 listed former members as dead, removed, or excommunicated *as of that date.* See Richard D. Pierce, ed. (with introduction by Robert E. Moody), *The Records of the First Church in Salem* . . . (Salem, 1974), pp. xxiv, 8.
3. Quoted by Winthrop S. Hudson in the introduction to his excellent edition of Williams, *Experiments of Spiritual Life & Health* (Philadelphia, 1951), p. 16.
4. *Ibid.,* pp. 93-94.
5. *Ibid.,* pp. 101, 103.
6. J. O. Austin, *The Genealogical Dictionary of Rhode Island* (Albany, 1887; reprinted Baltimore, 1969), pp. 103-104.

Section D.

1. John E. Pomfret, *The Province of East New Jersey, 1609-1702* (Princeton, 1962), pp. 42-44; Pomfret, *The Province of West New*

Notes

Jersey, 1609-1702 (Princeton, 1956), p. 274; Norman H. Maring, *Baptists in New Jersey* (Valley Forge, Pa., 1964), pp. 14f., 23, 38, 41, 74.

The following listing is drawn largely — though not exclusively — from J. O. Austin, *Genealogical Dictionary*, pp. 103-104.

(John?, "infant of Obadiah Hulmes of Redish" buried at Stockport, June 27, 1633)
1. Mary (?-1690+); married John Browne; 7 children
2. Martha (1640-1682+); married _____ Odlin
3. Samuel (1642-1679); married Alice Stillwell; 6 children
4. Obadiah (1644-1723); married _____ Cole; 5 children
5. Lydia (?-1682+); married John Bowne; 5 children
6. Jonathan (?-1713); married Sarah Borden; 9 children
7. John (1649-1712); married, Frances Holden; M. Greene; 9 children
8. Hopestill (?-between 1675 and 1681); married _____ Taylor
9. Joseph (?-1682+); mentioned in will; no other record

2. Pomfret, *East New Jersey*, pp. 44, 56, 96.
3. The discovery of the direct line from Holmes to Abraham Lincoln was made by Wilbur Nelson, who published a small booklet on the subject: *Obadiah Holmes, Ancestor and Prototype of Abraham Lincoln* (Newport, 1932). The chart below is found on page 2.

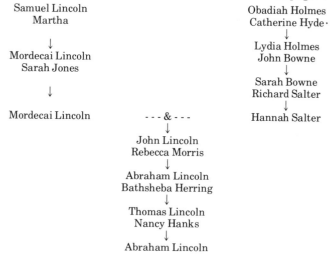

Samuel Lincoln   Obadiah Holmes
Martha   Catherine Hyde·
↓   ↓
Mordecai Lincoln   Lydia Holmes
Sarah Jones   John Bowne
↓   ↓
       Sarah Bowne
       Richard Salter
       ↓
Mordecai Lincoln   - - - & - - -   Hannah Salter
↓
John Lincoln
Rebecca Morris
↓
Abraham Lincoln
Bathsheba Herring
↓
Thomas Lincoln
Nancy Hanks
↓
Abraham Lincoln

See also William E. Barton, *The Lineage of Lincoln* (Indianapolis, 1929), pp. 43-45; and Ida M. Tarbell, *In the Footsteps of the Lincolns* (New York, 1924), pp. 32-34.

4. James B. Hedges, *The Browns of Providence Plantations: Colonial Years* (Cambridge, Mass., 1952). A portion of the chart found on p. 21 is given below:

John Browne (b. 1630) — Mary Holmes
↓
James Browne (b. 1666) — Mary Harris
↓
_____

Obadiah (b. 1712)   James (b. 1698) — Hope Power   Elisha (b. 1717)
↓
_____

James (b. 1724)   Nicholas (b. 1729)   Joseph (b. 1733)
            John (b. 1736)   Moses (b. 1738)

By the end of the nineteenth century, at least one dozen "Obadiah Brown's" occur in this lineage; see [A. I. Bulkley], *Chad Browne Memorial . . . 1638-1888* (Brooklyn, 1888).

5. *Early Records of the Town of Providence,* 21 vols. (Providence: 1892-1915), I, 17.

6. Newport Historical Society, Vault A, Box 50, Folder 9. Jonathan Holmes received one of the largest land grants in Monmouth County — 761 acres. He also served as captain of the Middletown (N.J.) militia in 1673. See Edwin P. Tanner, *The Province of New Jersey, 1664-1738* (New York, reprint 1967); and *Documents Relative to the Colonial History of New York* (Albany, 1858), II, 608.

7. Quoted in Gordon E. Geddes, "Welcome Joy! Death in Puritan New England, 1630-1730" (Ph. D. diss., University of California, Riverside, 1976), p. 136.

8. *Ibid.,* pp. 135-136.

9. *Ibid.,* p. 135.

Section E.

1. See the Records of the First Baptist Church, Swansea, in the Brown University Library, pp. 62, 90; John Russell, *A Brief Narrative . . .* (London, 1680), title page; Record Book of the First Baptist Church, Newport, in the Newport Historical Society.

2. Newport Historical Society, Vault A, Box 50, Folder 5.

3. *Ibid.*

4. The attitude of the Newport church toward communion and congregational singing is inferred in part from a long letter by William Hiscox and Samuel Hubbard to the Baptist church in Boston (Feb. 1, 1680). A portion of one sentence reads: ". . . it is not long since that you yourselves were as bad in their [Newport's] account for having to do with Mr. Myles [of the Swansea open-

communion church], & for singing of psalms, & to public worship with others." *Samuel Hubbard's Journal* (typescript, Providence, 1940), p. 116.
5. The full covenant has been printed in a booklet published by the Newport church, now the United Baptist Church, entitled *310 Years of Christian Service* (Newport, n. d.).

Section F.

1. The Geneva Bible went through 120 editions or reprintings between 1560 and 1611, and over 60 editions or reprintings after 1611 (though some of the latter were of the New Testament only). See the introduction by Lloyd E. Berry in *The Geneva Bible: A Facsimile of the 1560 Edition* (Madison, 1969).

   John Clarke's Bible, now in the possession of the Rhode Island Historical Society, is a 1608 edition of the Geneva Bible (printed in London by Robert Barker). A brief service book with the Psalms is bound in the front, and at the back may be found "Two right profitable and fruitful concordances, or large and ample tables alphabetical." This Bible, which apparently first belonged to John Clarke's father, Thomas (1570-1627), contains vital statistics pertinent to the Clarke family.
2. Berry, *The Geneva Bible.* Some of Holmes' biblical quotations do seem to owe more to the Geneva than to other translations, though it is impossible to insist upon this since, according to Berry, the Geneva Bible is the strongest single influence on the King James translation.

Section G.

1. Both the will and the inventory are in the Newport Historical Society, the former in Vault A, Box 103; the latter in Vault A, Box 50, Folder 9, #2.
2. Kenneth A. Lockridge, *Literacy in Colonial New England* (New York, 1974), p. 12.
3. John Clarke's will is framed and sometimes on exhibit in the Newport Historical Society.
4. See the modern edition by Bernard Bailyn, *The Apologia of Robert Keayne* [August 1, 1653] (New York, 1964).
5. The will of Robert Holmes, proved at Chester, October 11, 1698, declared as an initial concern: "First and principally, I commit my soul into the hands of Almighty God my Creator; steadfastly believing through the meritorious death and passion and from and by the merits and satisfaction of Jesus Christ, my Saviour

and Redeemer, to have full and free pardon and forgiveness of all
my sins and transgressions, and through the almighty power of
God at the last day to receive the same soul and body reunited and
made incorruptible, like Christ's glorious body, and with Him
and all the blessed to be made partakers of perfect bliss and glory
to all eternity." The will is now located in the Lancashire County
Record Office, Preston.

6. This deed is in the Newport Historical Society, Vault A, Box 50,
Folder 9, #3.

7. Obadiah himself was left £10 in his own father's will (proved at
Chester, Nov. 24, 1640; now also in Preston), but only on the
condition that a much younger son, Joseph, not survive to his own
maturity, i.e., twenty-one years of age. Obadiah's brother Robert
received the family farm in Reddish, while of another brother,
Samuel, the father wrote: "I give and bequeath to my son, Samuel
Hulme [Holmes], six shillings, eight pence, and no more, in
regard of the former great charges I have been put unto in and
about his education." Samuel was one of the Oxford-educated
brothers; see above, Ch. 1, p. 7; also p. 136, n.9.

8. In the inventory of the estate of Robert Holmes, one cow is
appraised at a value of £3, 13 s., and another at £3, 10 s.; a horse is
valued at £4. In the inventory printed above, two mares and a colt
are collectively valued at £4, 10 s. Of course, in no instance does
one know anything of the age or condition of the animals, but
some general sense of the real value of the bequests and of the
estate can be reckoned.

A Note on the Sources

BY FAR THE MOST VALUABLE MATERIALS FOR THIS STUDY ARE located in the Newport Historical Society. These include the Record Book of the First Baptist Church, copied or collected by John Comer early in the eighteenth century; the Testimony of Obadiah Holmes, his last will, two deeds, and the inventory of his estate; and other papers relating to the Holmes family and to the Baptists in seventeenth-century Newport. Without these manuscripts, of course, this book would not have been possible. Other manuscript materials I used are found in the Rhode Island Historical Society, Brown University Library, Massachusetts Historical Society, the Backus Collection of Andover Newton Theological School, and the Lancashire Record Office in Preston, England. Specific titles and locations have been indicated in the notes above.

Of the seventeenth-century materials that found their way into print at the time, the two most valuable items are John Clarke's *Ill Newes from New-England* . . . (London, 1652) and Thomas Cobbet's *The Civil Magistrates Power* . . . (London, 1653). The latter is available in a modern facsimile reprint (New York, 1972), while Clarke's treatise is accessible in the *Collections of the Massachusetts Historical Society,* Fourth Series, Vol. II (1854). The publication of much other primary data did not come until the nineteenth or twentieth centuries in the form of town and colony records or annals. Those I used most frequently include the following: John Russell Bartlett, ed., *Records of the Colony of Rhode Island*

and *Providence Plantations in New England,* 10 vols. (Providence, 1856-1865); Nathaniel B. Shurtleff, ed., *Records of the Colony of New Plymouth in New England,* 12 vols. (Boston, 1855-1861); Shurtleff, ed., *Records of the Governor and Company of the Massachusetts Bay in New England,* 5 vols. (Boston, 1853-1854); Joseph B. Felt, *Annals of Salem,* 2 vols., second edition (Salem: 1845, 1849); and Richard LeBaron Bowen, *Early Rehoboth,* 4 vols. (Rehoboth, 1945-1950). For the early years of Newport, one may consult the series of articles by Lloyd A. Robson beginning in Vol. 37 (1964) of *Newport History,* a bulletin of the Newport Historical Society. Certain court and other legal records have been cited in the notes, as have the collected writings of specific individuals (e.g., the *Winthrop Papers,* and the *Complete Writings of Roger Williams*).

The secondary literature of greatest utility pertains either to the Baptists or to the colony of Rhode Island. From the English side, the path-breaking works of Champlin Burrage, *The Early English Dissenters . . .,* 2 vols. (Cambridge, 1912); and Wilbur K. Jordan, *The Development of Religious Toleration in England,* 4 vols. (London, 1932-1940) continue to prove their worth. On the American side, the Baptist historian Isaac Backus provided the first careful treatment of the origin and development of the denomination in the colonies: *A History of New England, with Particular Reference to the Denomination of Christians called Baptists,* 2 vols., 2nd edition (Newton, Mass., 1871; reprint New York, 1969). Alone among Baptist historians, Backus made a serious effort to carve a niche in history for Obadiah Holmes. William G. McLoughlin, in his massive study of *New England Dissent, 1630-1833: The Baptists and the Separation of Church and State,* 2 vols. (Cambridge, Mass., 1971), elevated the religious historiography of the Baptists in colonial New England to a new plane. Otherwise, denominational history for Holmes' time and place is limited in value. The best history of an individual church is Nathan E. Wood, *The History of the First Baptist Church of Boston, 1665-1899* (Philadelphia, 1899); for the Newport and Providence churches, only brief treatments are available: C. E. Barrows, *Historical Sketch of the First Baptist Church, Newport, Rhode Island* (Newport, 1876); and the opening pages of Henry Melville King, *Historical Catalogue of the Members of the First Baptist Church in Providence, Rhode Island* (Providence, 1908). Wilbur Nelson, who became pastor of the Newport Church in 1919, wrote a short biography of Clarke (*The Hero of Aquidneck: A Life of Dr. John Clarke* [New York, 1938]) as well as a small pamphlet on Holmes (*Obadiah Holmes, Ancestor and Prototype of Abraham Lincoln* [Newport, 1932]).

With respect to the colonial history of Rhode Island, it will be sufficient to mention only the first and the last ventures in a long series. John Callendar, pastor of the Newport church from 1731 until his death in 1748, published *An Historical Discourse, on the Civil and Religious Affairs of the Colony of Rhode-Island and Providence Plantations . . .* (Boston, 1739; reprint Freeport, N.Y., 1971); though only a brief review, it still has value for an understanding of the seventeenth century. The most recent history, Sydney V. James, *Colonial Rhode Island: A History* (New York, 1975), fortunately makes it unnecessary to expand this Note on the Sources with respect to the early history of Rhode Island. James' extensive and critical bibliography, pp. 385-411, offers fresh and expert guidance under topical headings.

For the early years and background of Obadiah Holmes, the publications of the Chetham Society and the Lancashire and Cheshire Antiquarian Society have proved most helpful. The former published three elaborate series, entitled *Remains Historical & Literary connected with the Palatine Counties of Lancaster and Cheshire* (114 volumes in the First Series, 110 in the "New Series," and an ongoing Third Series which began in 1949). The *Transactions of the Lancashire and Cheshire Antiquarian Society,* also published in Manchester, consist of annual volumes beginning in 1884. Of New England's several major historical societies, the publications of the following have been of particular value: the Massachusetts Historical Society (both the *Collections* and the

Proceedings), the New England Historical and Genealogical Society, the Colonial Society of Massachusetts, the Essex Institute, the American Antiquarian Society, and the Rhode Island Historical Society.

Index

165

Index

Index

quoted, 4; relationship with Clarke and Holmes, 144 n.25, 144 n.27; Rhode Island charter, securing of, 42; Salem period, 11-12; Seventh Day, views on, 150 n.37; unpopularity of, 152 n.46; wife of, 93-94
Willis, John, 143 n.19
Wilson, John, 27, 35, 142 n.17
Winslow, Edward, 142 n.14

Winslow, Ola E., 136 n.12, 154 n.5
Winthrop, John, 10, 16, 136-37 n.18, 141 n.12
Winthrop, John, Jr., 17, 48, 67, 68, 149 n.19
Witter, William, 22, 23
Wood, Nathan E., 148 n.16, 154 n.3
Woodley, Edward, 142-43 n.19
Worship, service of, 24, 106, 157-58 n.4